PLATE 1

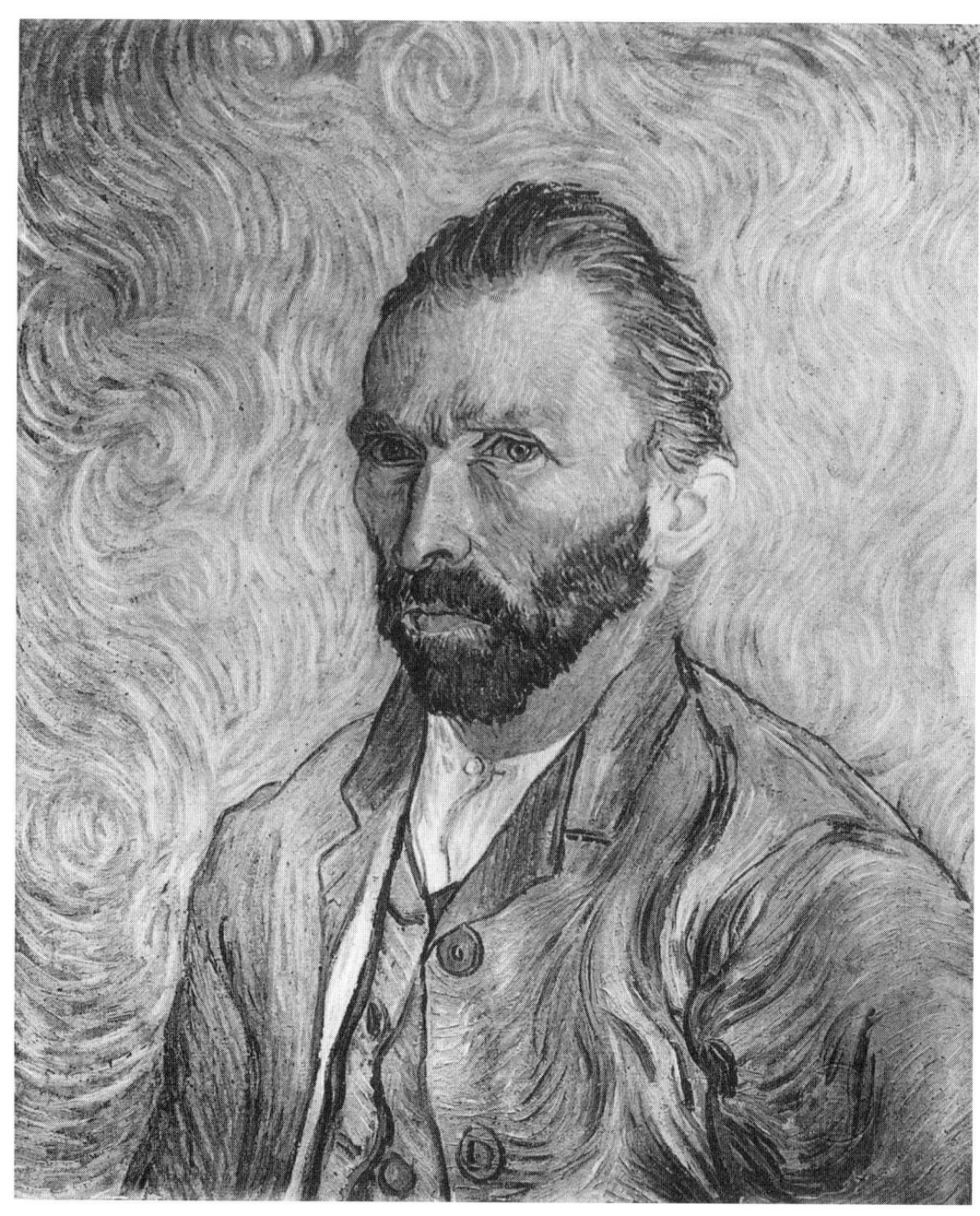

SELF-PORTRAIT OF VINCENT VAN GOGH

VAN GOGH ON ART AND ARTISTS
LETTERS TO EMILE BERNARD

Vincent van Gogh

Edited and Translated by
DOUGLAS LORD

DOVER PUBLICATIONS, INC.
Mineola, New York

ERRATA

Corrections

Page x, plate 24   *for:* on loan to Boston Art Gallery *read:* on loan to Museum of Fine Arts, Boston.

Page 30, l. 16   *for:* when will they have seen enough of him *read:* when will we have seen enough of him.

Page 44, l. 19   *for:* and yet relieves our despair *read:* which arouses our despair.

Page 45, l. 14   *for:* though he disdained books written about ideas *read:* though he disdained to write books about ideas.

Page 74, l. 29   *for:* Further, I am attempting some dusty thistles *read:* Next, I'm looking for some dusty thistles. *Vide Letters to Theo, No. 526.*

Page 95, note 5   *should read: Vide* Letter 540 to Theo: "For the second time I have scraped off a study of Christ with the angel in the garden of olives." The first time would be the occasion mentioned in Letter 505.

D. L.

Bibliographical Note

This Dover edition, first published in 2003, is an unabridged republication of the work originally published in 1938 by the Museum of Modern Art, New York, under the title *Vincent Van Gogh: Letters to Emile Bernard.* The French version of which this is the translation was published in 1911 by Ambroise Vollard, Paris.

Library of Congress Cataloging-in-Publication Data

Gogh, Vincent van, 1853-1890.
    [Lettres de Vincent van Gogh à Emile Bernard. English]
    Van Gogh on art and artists: letters to Emile Bernard / Vincent van Gogh; edited, translated, and with a foreword by Douglas Lord.—Dover ed.
        p. cm.
    Originally published: Letters to Emile Bernard. New York : Museum of Modern Art, 1938.
    Includes index.
    ISBN 0-486-42727-7 (pbk.)
    1. Gogh, Vincent van, 1853-1890—Correspondence. 2. Bernard, Emile, 1868-1941—Correspondence. 3. Painters—Netherlands—Correspondence. 4. Painters—France—Correspondence. 5. Art—Themes, motives. I. Lord, Douglas, 1911- II. Title.

ND653.G7 A3 2003
759.9492—dc21
[B]

2002072876

Manufactured in the United States of America
Dover Publications, Inc., 31 East 2nd Street, Mineola, N.Y. 11501

ACKNOWLEDGEMENTS

My thanks are due to Ing. V. W. van Gogh for his generous permission to publish the present English translation; to the Baroness de Goldschmidt-Rothschild for her kindness in allowing me to consult and photograph the manuscript originals in her possession; to my friend Mr. Alfred Barr for his great interest and his endless helpful suggestions; to M. Emile Bernard for various information and for supplying me with a photograph; to M. Smirnov, Director of VOKS in Moscow, and to Dr. Gruyter for supplying me with photographs.

Acknowledgements are also due to M. Emile Bernard for permission to quote from his writings; also to the Directors of Rijksmuseum Kröller-Müller, Museum Folkwang and Museum of Modern Western Art in Moscow for permission to reproduce paintings in these galleries.

DOUGLAS LORD

CONTENTS

ACKNOWLEDGEMENTS   *page* v

LIST OF PLATES   ix

INTRODUCTION   1

A NOTE ON EMILE BERNARD   12

LETTER   I   [Paris: Spring 1887]   19

        II   [Arles: March 1888]   22

       III   [Arles: early April 1888]   24

        IV   [Arles: about 20th April 1888]   26

         V   [Arles: late May 1888]   30

        VI   [Arles: mid-June 1888]   34

       VII   [Arles: about 20th June 1888]   38

      VIII   [Arles: last week of June 1888]   44

        IX   [Arles: last week of June 1888]   50

         X   [Arles: about 14th July 1888]   54

        XI   [Arles: about 20th July 1888]   57

       XII   [Arles: late July 1888]   59

      XIII   [Arles: late July 1888]   63

       XIV   [Arles: early August 1888]   68

        XV   [Arles: mid-August 1888]   74

       XVI   [Arles: mid-September 1888]   77

      XVII   [Arles: late September 1888]   80

     XVIII   [Arles: late September 1888]   83

       XIX   [Arles: beginning of October 1888]   88

        XX   [St. Rémy: mid-October 1889]   92

       XXI   [St. Rémy: mid-November 1889]   96

      XXII   to *Gauguin* [Arles: mid-October 1888]   104

     XXIII   *Gauguin* to *Bernard* [Arles: November 1888]   106

CHRONOLOGY   108

SELECT BIBLIOGRAPHY   111

COMPARATIVE TABLE OF LETTER NUMBERS   114

EMENDATIONS TO THE PUBLISHED TEXT   115

INDEX   121

PLATES

1 SELF-PORTRAIT (1890) by Vincent van Gogh *Frontispiece*
Collection Dr. Gachet, Auvers
Photo Vizzavona, Paris

2 PORTRAIT OF EMILE BERNARD (1886) *at page* 12
by Henri de Toulouse-Lautrec
Collection Ambroise Vollard, Paris

3 Facsimile from LETTER II 22

4 THE DRAWBRIDGE NEAR ARLES (March 1888) 22
Collection V. W. van Gogh, Laren
Photo Vizzavona, Paris

5 Facsimile from LETTER III 24

6 A PROVENÇAL ORCHARD (April 1888) 24
Collection Rijksmuseum Kröller-Müller, Hoenderlô
Photo Vizzavona, Paris

7 Facsimile from LETTER IV 27
Photo Dora Maar, Paris

8 A PROVENÇAL ORCHARD (April 1888) 27
Collection Albert Stern, Amsterdam

9 VAN GOGH'S HOUSE AT ARLES (September 1888) 30
Collection V. W. van Gogh, Laren
Photo Museum of Modern Art, New York

10 Facsimile from LETTER VI 33
Photo Dora Maar, Paris

11 STILL LIFE WITH COFFEE-POT (May 1888) 33
Collection Thea Sternheim, Paris
Photo Vizzavona, Paris

12 Facsimile from LETTER VI 34
Photo Dora Maar, Paris

13 Facsimile from LETTER VI (verso of Plate 10) 37
Photo Dora Maar, Paris

14 BOATS ON THE BEACH AT SAINTES-MARIES (June 1888)   *at page* 37
Collection V. W. van Gogh, Laren
Photo Vizzavona, Paris

15 Facsimile from LETTER VI (verso of Plate 17)   39
Photo Dora Maar, Paris

16 BOATS ON THE SEA AT SAINTES-MARIES (June 1888)   39
Collection Museum of Modern Western Art, Moscow
Photo Museum of Modern Western Art

17 Facsimile from LETTER VI   41
Photo Dora Maar, Paris

18 HOUSES AT SAINTES-MARIES (June 1888)   41
Photo Vizzavona, Paris

19 Facsimile from LETTER VII   43
Photo Dora Maar, Paris

20 THE SOWER (June 1888)   43
Collection Rijksmuseum Kröller-Müller, Hoenderlô

21 Facsimile from LETTER VII (verso of Plate 19)   45
Photo Dora Maar, Paris

22 VIEW OF ARLES AT SUNSET (June 1888)   45
Collection Winterthur Museum
Photo H. Linck, Winterthur

23 THE ZOUAVE (June 1888)   46
Photo Vizzavona, Paris

24 THE POSTMAN ROULIN (August 1888)   70
Collection Robert Treat Paine 2nd (On loan to Boston Art Gallery)
Photo Museum of Modern Art, New York

25 THE NIGHT CAFÉ (September 1888)   78
Collection Stephen C. Clark, New York
Photo Museum of Modern Art, New York

26 Facsimile from LETTER XXI   96
Photo Dora Maar, Paris

27 THE GARDEN OF THE ASYLUM AT SAINT-RÉMY (October 1889)   98
Collection Museum Folkwang, Essen
Photo Museum Folkwang, Essen

28 A REAPER AT WORK IN A WHEATFIELD AT SAINT-RÉMY (October 1889) *at page* 100
Collection Rijksmuseum Kröller-Müller, Hoenderlô
Photo Vizzavona, Paris

29 Facsimile from LETTER XXII   105
Photo Dora Maar, Paris

30 VAN GOGH'S BEDROOM AT ARLES (October 1888)   105
Collection Art Institute of Chicago (Birch-Bartlett collection)
Photo Museum of Modern Art, New York

31 Facsimile from LETTER XXIII: letter from Gauguin to Emile Bernard   106
Photo Dora Maar, Paris

32 Facsimile from LETTER XXIII (verso of Plate 31)   107
Photo Dora Maar, Paris

xi

INTRODUCTION

The present volume is, so far as we know, the only collection of van Gogh Letters not previously translated into English. It is also a most important collection: for not only does it show us an intensely human side of van Gogh, but, being letters to another artist, they give us a deeper insight into the technical problems with which he was concerned.

There can be little doubt that Vincent was a picturesque, even eccentric, personality, and this has cost him dear. Much that has been published about him is both inaccurate and fictitious. That is why his own letters are such a valuable source of information. However Emile Bernard is an outstanding exception, and of his early writings about his friend I can only speak with the greatest admiration; as a more or less contemporary estimate of Vincent, man, artist, and friend, they are, apart from being almost unique, possibly still among the most sensitive and understanding studies ever published. Admittedly Bernard is not always strictly accurate: in the first French edition of this Correspondence, for example, many of the letters were wrongly dated and arranged. But at that time much of the detail of van Gogh's life was scarcely known; in fact Bernard himself has admitted that it was not until long after Vincent's death that he first heard of his work in the Borinage. As early as 1893 Bernard was assisting in the publication of selected letters to Theo, as well as of parts of the present volume; it was Bernard who, after Theo's death, attempted to preserve and collect all the papers in the latter's possession, amongst which were his own letters to Vincent; again it was to Bernard that, in 1890, Theo turned for help with the arrangement of Vincent's pictures in his studio; it was Bernard too who was responsible for the organisation of the first van Gogh exhibition in Paris. Such was the enthusiasm of the young man to whom the following letters were addressed, and to whom more than anyone else van Gogh's early recognition was due.

But, unfortunately, not all Vincent's commentators have had the same spirit of sympathetic honesty, so that the growth of the van Gogh

1

legend is a most provocative study. In editing the present volume, I have relied almost entirely on the three volumes of Vincent's letters to Theo, which are of course our most direct and reliable source of information and which present the reader with an amazingly complete picture of the detail of his life. After leaving Paris he wrote to Theo as a rule at least two or three times a week and sometimes twice in one day. Probably only a few people will read every word in these three large tomes, for they are full of intimate details and problems which are more of interest to art-historians and to fellow-craftsmen. Yet it is a wonderfully human and moving document and no praise can be too lavish for the amazingly careful editing of Mme. van Gogh-Bonger or for the excellence of her translation. There is scarcely a mistake in the chronological arrangement of these letters and thus they form an absolute touchstone, as well as a standard by which to work. None of the following letters was actually dated by Vincent himself: all dates have been supplied tentatively by myself after careful collation with the *Letters to Theo* and are therefore enclosed within brackets.

However in the study of the art of van Gogh the rôle of his correspondence must not be exaggerated. It is perhaps difficult in his particular case to separate the man from the artist, yet this is what we must do in fairness to the artist. Admittedly his work depends in some measure for its greater effect on an intimate knowledge of what he wrote about it. It is ultimately important—the importance being relative to our immediate reactions in front of the canvas—to know that in the picture of his BEDROOM AT ARLES he wanted "to express a feeling of perfect rest". Art, for him, was a matter of more than pure æsthetics: "in a picture I want to say something comforting as music is comforting, I want to paint men and women with that something of the eternal which the halo used to symbolise, and which we seek to give by the actual radiance and vibration of our colourings". But this is something to be read after we have looked at the picture not before.

Our knowledge of the private lives of artists should in general play no part in our appreciation of their work: this should exist alone, as impersonally as a Chou bronze or a Byzantine mosaic. Van Gogh

2

however is one of the artists whose work must be excepted, but it has been his misfortune to have his story turned into a cheap literary sensation at the expense of a proper interest in his art. That is why it seems to me more important than ever to insist today on the fact that even his pictures both can and should be looked at for themselves alone and that they are made no more comprehensible by the highly decorated anecdotes that are woven into his life. If van Gogh the artist is to retain a great position in our estimation it will be purely on artistic grounds. In our study of van Gogh the artist his correspondence should be but an element: in our study of van Gogh the man it is of the utmost importance.

Of van Gogh the artist so much has already been written that I need add little here, though it seems to me that his essentially northern and teutonic character has not been sufficiently emphasised. The following letters betray it clearly in his passionate love of the earth and the peasants, his animal ferocity, the violence of his reaction to the South and its colour, as well as in his emphatic, moral severity: his excitement is spontaneous and certainly overwhelming. There is nothing Latin, nothing Mediterranean about van Gogh: he came from the cold and comfortless North and was blinded by the South and its luxuriance. I have never been able to understand why he is so consistently labelled "French School". It is true that his two years in Paris had an enormous influence on his development, but no French painter, even an out-and-out Romantic such as Delacroix, ever dared paint with so little restraint. Or should I, perhaps, with greater accuracy say ever needed to paint with so little restraint: the Latin races are more naturally emotional.

His break with Impressionism was inevitable. Impressionism as a technique of painting was only possible in the atmospheric North. Renoir's crisis of 1881, when he turned to Ingres, was largely brought on by his contact with the South; Cézanne, a Southerner, sought to make of Impressionism something solid like the art of the museums; van Gogh in LETTER III says "I try to secure the essential in the drawing—then I go for the spaces, bounded by contours, either expressed or not". The peculiarity of the South is its hard petrifying light, which isolates every detail of a landscape giving pronounced outlines, so that mountains really look like terrifying piles of solid rock, trees like shapes in cast iron and the sun like a blazing fiery orb. The heat and light of the sun run like a refrain through these letters. Cézanne with his fear of contours and his obsession with tonal modulation is not really a painter of the South: though I would say that it was his southern origin which forced him to insist on solidity. But van Gogh was the first painter ever to come so near a realisation of southern conditions and I suggest that this was due to his northern origin. From the following letters, and particularly from Nos. XII and XIII, it is clear that he himself was acutely conscious of the extraordinary penetration of his vision as a foreigner. But he had to record immediately his emotions, before they could be corrected by his intellect: "I regret sometimes that I can't make up my mind to work more at home and from memory. The imagination . . . alone can bring us to the creation of a more exalting and consoling nature than we are shown in a solitary glance at reality." He did not sit down and think out his composition through a progression of sketches and more complete drawings; he worked directly in paint on canvas except at times when he was too poor to afford the expense. This explains the enormous quantity of his production: during the time between his arrival in Paris in March 1886 and his death in July 1890 he was able to produce over 600 paintings: that is to say slightly less than Cézanne's output in a period ten times as long, and about four times that of Seurat (including all his small sketches) in the space of ten years.

Van Gogh of course is a painter with a message: he is preoccupied with the purpose of life and is in this sense the artistic counterpart of a novelist like Zola; hence his emphasis on the content rather than the form of his pictures. He is what is called an Expressionist painter, and that accounts for his subsequent influence being so much greater on German than on French art. He did not look at and accept life as it is, but thought always of what he might do to alter or improve it. There is none of the classical balance and restraint in his work, none of the French placidity. He is far removed from the reasoned perfection of a Poussin, the delicate grace of a Watteau or the aristocratic romanticism of a Delacroix: he is much nearer to *Sturm und Drang*. One can see it for

4

example in what he writes of Cézanne in the following pages: temperamentally these two artists were irreconcilable, and, although painting much the same subjects, incapable of mutual understanding. There is further evidence of this in what Cézanne wrote some years later to Emile Bernard:[1] "You have, I think, only to continue along this line [laid down by Cézanne], you have understood what you must do and you will soon be turning your back on the Gauguins and van Goghs". Cézanne, being thoroughly French, submitted his emotions to the control of a keen, logical intellect: he was a good, solid bourgeois, as Vincent says, eminently sane, building up a picture slowly, deliberately and with the maximum of exactitude in the tones, yet never, as he thought, quite able fully to realise his sensations. Van Gogh was impulsive, intensely emotional, mystic and unbalanced: he painted as it were "red hot", intuitively and ferociously—a hit or miss method. The unity of his pictures is not so much a visual as a spiritual unity. But then as Mr. Herbert Read says:[2] "Art is not the expression in plastic form of any one particular ideal. It is the expression of any ideal which the artist can realise in plastic form. And though I think that every work of art has some principle of form or coherent structure I would not stress this element in any obvious sense, because the more one studies the structure of works of art which live in virtue of their direct and instinctive appeal, the more difficult it becomes to reduce them to simple and explicable formulæ." Yet pictures which appeal directly to our emotions and do not also appeal to our intellect tend to have but little lasting value. That is why it is important today that our direct reactions to van Gogh's pictures should not be the result of undue sentiment. Vincent was anti-intellectual, but not on the whole a sentimental artist: and by sentimentality in art I mean that the artist's emotions are disproportionate to their cause. He must be accounted successful if he can really make us feel the genuineness of the emotions which he wished to communicate. Every work of art should be judged individually on its æsthetic merits. The acceptance of this as the

[1] *Vide Paul Cézanne: Correspondence,* edited by John Rewald (Grasset, Paris 1938), Letter 167.

[2] *Vide The Meaning of Art,* by Herbert Read (Faber, London 1931), p. 5.

5

ultimate test renders the artist's avowed intentions of no importance. It is what he did, not what he meant to do, which matters. We must learn to rely on our eyes.

Of van Gogh the man much has also been written. Of his essential humanity the following letters, with their recurring theme of Bernard's health and military service, can best be left to speak for themselves. Any point which it has seemed to me might be obscure has been explained in the Notes at the end of each letter. But as a matter of interest I should like to quote at length Emile Bernard's own story of the original publication, written specially as a Preface to the 1911 edition:

"In 1892, not long after the death of van Gogh, my friendship urged on me the imperious duty of making known to the world the mind of one who had been my dearest colleague, and of whose affectionate devotion I had so often had proof. So I spoke to Paul Fort of the letters from Vincent in my possession and, indeed, showed them to him. At first he was attracted by the pretty drawings which were scattered among the script, then by the passages which I read to him: so much so that he communicated his enthusiasm to M. Alfred Vallette, director of the *Mercure de France*. M. Alfred Vallette, with the initiative and intelligence for which he is famous, at once decided to ask me to allow these letters to be published. 'I have been told,' he wrote, 'that you possess some letters from van Gogh illustrated with drawings and sketches, and that you would gladly allow their publication. Now on the one hand the *Mercure* was one of the first to interest itself in van Gogh, and on the other hand it is, I believe, one of the most widely read *avant-garde* publications, both in France and abroad, so don't you think that these letters would be best placed with us?' I did not wait to be asked, as you may well imagine, before handing over these epistles from my friend who had died unknown, for I hoped thus to repair something of the unjust neglect he had suffered in this world. After an exhibition which I was alone in organising, after the silence of the press and of his friends, the only thing left for me to do was to try and stimulate appreciation of Vincent by revealing his mind, his struggle and his life.

"His letters were the most potent means. After reading them one could not doubt his sincerity, his character, nor his originality; there, pulsating with life, one would find the whole of him.

"But a selection had to be made among these letters, which were confidential notes from one friend to another, in which details of private life are mixed up with matters of art and which too publicly expose both the person to whom they are addressed as well as his circle. It was a question of picking out and putting into relief the passages most likely to arouse interest. Rather than publish them in their entirety it was better to extract only the essence, so to speak, and thus, by a careful and calculated introduction of van Gogh's mind to the great public, attain the desired end. In the extracts published in the *Mercure de France* I decided to print nothing which, by its harshness of language or crudity of expression, could possibly hurt anyone: I decided to print no reference to myself, and only to give the initials of those of our friends who were involved in our life at that time.

"To-day there is no more reason for such caution. Success (a ridiculous word which has a meaning in this particular context) blessed the Letters of Vincent van Gogh to Emile Bernard and to his brother Theodore and has at the same time borne his pictures as far as the museums of Germany and Holland. These letters, henceforth of historic importance for the art of our time, have already appeared in a German edition: others too, perhaps—done, like that one, without my knowledge—may have helped to spread the fame of Vincent throughout Europe. It merely remained for me, bowing to the ever-growing desire of several artisits, to make known all I knew of van Gogh's life and to publish his correspondence with me *in extenso*.

"Here it is. This time nothing is omitted.[1]

"His grammatical errors: his continual *ici, mais, cela, en tant que quant à, maintenant*, etc., the clumsy, child-like, foreign turn of phrase, through which the thought nevertheless comes effectively, his language with its flashes of tenderness, gracefulness and goodness, sometimes taking wing, sometimes plunging into the vulgar expressions of Parisian studios or into the slang of brothels—his language, I say, needs no excuses, sympathy with it is assured because, despite all the well-worn idioms which trip it up, the waves of alcohol in which it swims, the realism of the prose which taints it, it bursts suddenly, unexpectedly upon a meadow brilliant with sunlight or flowers, a silent town in which is reflected a star-spangled sky, a world unknown resounding with the word of Christ, echoing with the music of art. At once both human and religious, he blends the ugliness of our hell with the spiritual graces of Redemption and Glory. The colours which he so often names and whose sequence he recites like a litany, like some mystic chaplet, adorn his language with their jewels just as drops of water after a storm glisten over the muddy acres of ploughed land. Dutch by birth, Vincent became French through love of our country-side, though he really appreciated the climate more than the traditions. He never spoke of our cathedrals, of our Gothic period, of our Grand Siècle: in fact, he here

---

[1] This is not absolutely accurate. Bernard himself, it is true, wanted to publish the whole text, but at the last minute M. Vollard for personal reasons, partly on account of Degas, saw fit to omit several words, not to mention whole sentences and paragraphs, now listed here in an Appendix. This, therefore, is the first absolutely complete version of the text.

admits that he detests the 'Roi-Soleil'. But what he loved was our actual sun, our well-ordered life. He was so much interested in us that in his paintings and descriptions of us it is always the most popular aspect he seizes on, always our most brilliant landscapes. What matter, then, if his style is not correct: it is alive and we can well indulge our delicate attention, for we are in contact with one of those superior beings who command it, even though they cannot speak our own language.

" 'Isn't it rather the intensity of thought than the tranquillity of touch we are after?' he writes. What he says about his painting, which seems in advance to excuse its disorder, his rather mad enthusiasm, can also be applied to his writing. It is the thought which we must get at, the true life which we must discover. There is certainly no tranquillity of touch there; but what intensity! And what pleasure these letters can give us after all the stylistic exhibitions we have suffered from people who have nothing to say.

"Ardour has no need of syntax nor of punctuation when it reaches the state of moral intoxication, of meditation and creation."

It is above all the record of his life and thought that he sets down pell-mell in this volume, and in the other volumes of his letters. In fact few, if any, artists can be followed so closely into their privacy, and over such a long period as van Gogh. By reading the letters one can follow not only his own troubles and worries, but actually many of the troubles of his time, both economic and spiritual. Unfortunately, of the letters he himself received, only one small collection from Theo has survived.[1] It is a great pity that Bernard's letters, for example, all of which we know he kept, should have been destroyed: just as it is a still greater pity that the only account of the unfortunate incident in Arles should be Gauguin's, for there is scarcely a word written by him whose truth has not at some time or other been seriously doubted. Altogether Gauguin's behaviour to van Gogh is one of the more sordid episodes of the period. From the letters to Bernard we see the position he held in Vincent's estimation: Vincent was prepared to place himself under Gauguin's leadership in the formation of a Southern school of Impressionist painters, and the lack of response to such a compliment in someone so overweeningly vain as Gauguin is certainly remarkable. Vincent was entirely responsible for encouraging Theo to buy from Gauguin, and indeed no sooner did the brothers hear that he was

[1] *Vide* Bibliography.

8

financially embarrassed than they dispatched what for them, considering that neither of them really had enough for their own needs, must have been large sums. Gauguin is probably much to blame for the crisis at Arles. He might, for all the jealousy, vanity and unrelenting egotism of his character, have been more considerate in his treatment of a friend whose health and nerves he found destroyed through overwork, hardship and under-nourishment and whose admiration was generous enough to follow him even after their separation. Yet Gauguin's expression of gratitude took the form of a distinctly twisted account of their relationship, and when asked by Bernard to help in the organisation of the first exhibition in Paris all he did was to send de Haan, one of his cronies, specially to prevent such a project maturing, on the grounds that it would not be politic from his (Gauguin's) point of view to allow an exhibition of the works of a madman. The exhibition was held nevertheless, thanks to Bernard, though de Haan did succeed in muzzling the press.

It was probably as a result of Vincent's unfortunate experiences with the women he loved that he tended to build up such strong attachments as he had to Theo, to Rappard, to Gauguin and to Bernard. Yet even the story of these friendships is strange. From Theo he was continually demanding more money. With van Rappard the friendship did not begin too well and it ended suddenly when this artist received THE POTATO EATERS with some scorn. "Perhaps it is just as well that all this happened," Vincent replied, "as I think it will be long before you again upbraid me and, as you call it, 'waver in your confidence'. I have had the same disagreeable contacts with a number of people—and for a number of years. Whenever I protested things became worse, and they would not listen to me. There are my parents and relatives, Teersteeg, and many people I knew when I was at Goupil's; they went so far in their disapproval of everything I did, that in the last couple of years, instead of wasting my time in trying to convince them (I have so little time to lose), I made short work of it and turned my back on them. *And I let them think and say whatever they liked, without bothering about it.* So this affair with you does not stand on its own feet, in case you think so. You have been bullied into it by public opinion. If you can now see that to be the fact, and think it over a little, then I want to state again that it may be a good thing that we have quarrelled a bit. But I insist on my point: I will not let the thing drag along in this way, nor do I want a dragged out friendship. Either it is sincere—or it is nothing."[1] With Gauguin there came disaster: and even with Bernard there was a crisis over his quotation from Baudelaire. Van Gogh's sympathy was immense and genuine, but his impetuousness and his unbending principles made any sustained relationship difficult. He did not know compromise: his criticisms of Bernard's pictures as well as of his poems show that. People were afraid of his austerity. He suffered always from a self-imposed isolation, which seems to have been psychological and which arose from his fear of succumbing to external influences, of not being wholly true to himself, of being forced to compromise. For this reason he lost almost every friend he made, yet in times of trouble, and when his mind was unusually disturbed, he generally tried to solve his difficulties by reaching out for friends, for human contacts. It was in this sort of mood that he proposed the union of southern Impressionist painters, for he could be as lavish in the sharing of his artistic knowledge and discoveries as he was with the little cash which he received from Theo.

Today I think but few people would still persist in seeing madness in van Gogh's pictures. He was subject certainly to periodic fits of varying intensity and duration, which came on quite suddenly and unexpectedly: but in the intervening periods there is ample evidence of his usual mental acuity, as we see in a painting like THE GARDEN OF THE ASYLUM AT SAINT-RÉMY (Plate 27) as well as in LETTERS XX and XXI and in the later ones to Theo. A long and varied list of mental diseases has been diagnosed to explain his case: masked and alcoholic epilepsy, epileptic hallucinations, schizzophrenia, paralysis after syphilis, terebic and solar intoxication, acute mania with general delirium and meningo-encephalitis. But none of these explanations are satisfactory. During most of his life van Gogh seems to have been the victim of a psychic disturbance. It drove him to the Borinage, it finally compelled him, after failure in wordly directions as art-dealer, theological student and

[1] *Letters to an Artist*, No. 57, p. 210.

10

preacher, to turn to art. But the point is that it was not his "madness" which drove him to artistic creation: even Dr. Jaspers, who diagnoses schizzophrenia, admits that this malady is not in itself creative. The gift of artistic creation was already latent in him, its liberation came as the inevitable result of some inner reorientation. In his worst moments van Gogh's state may have amounted to temporary madness, though the most probable explanation of the facts seems to be that he was simply what is now called "manic depressive".

Vincent lived and died for his work, it was his only consolation. Nothing would have made him happier than to hear Picasso say: "Why do the Dutch mourn for Rembrandt? They have van Gogh."

London 21st June 1938   DOUGLAS LORD

11

A NOTE ON EMILE BERNARD

Emile Bernard was born at Lille on 28th April 1868. In 1878 his family moved to Paris, where he was sent to study at the Collège Ste. Barbe. In 1885 he entered the studio of Fernand Cormon (1845-1924), an academic painter, to study painting. Here he made the acquaintance of Toulouse-Lautrec and Anquetin, who were fellow pupils: and it was at the end of 1885 that Lautrec painted the portrait of Bernard (Plate 2). This picture, according to Bernard, took thirty-three sittings to complete, ten of which were entirely devoted to working on the background. But he did not stay long at Cormon's, as he was found one day painting a nude in streaks of emerald and vermilion. Cormon threw him out of the studio saying he could not correct such things, sent for his father and asked for the removal of young Emile who was accused of having 'mis le désordre' in the studio. Thereupon, after a great scene, Emile's palette and box of colours were unceremoniously burnt by his father and he was confronted with entering the family business. He decided to run away from home, but, being caught in the act by his mother, was restrained and eventually agreed to the proposal that in April he should be free to leave and continue his painting. This in fact became an annual tour, on foot, a knapsack on his back: it lasted from April till October.

On 1st April 1886 Bernard set off on foot, leaving his family, to paint in Normandy and Brittany. On his way through Paris he stopped at Cormon's to say goodbye to his friends: there he saw a strange young man painting pictures, dark brown in colour, at which everyone was laughing. This was Vincent van Gogh, who had just arrived from Holland. But Bernard did not speak to him. It was not until 1887, when they met one day in the little shop of Père Tanguy, that their great friendship began.

On arriving at Concarneau, in Brittany, he found a man on the beach painting who, during the course of the ensuing conversation, spoke in glowing terms of the work of a painter called Gauguin who

PLATE 2

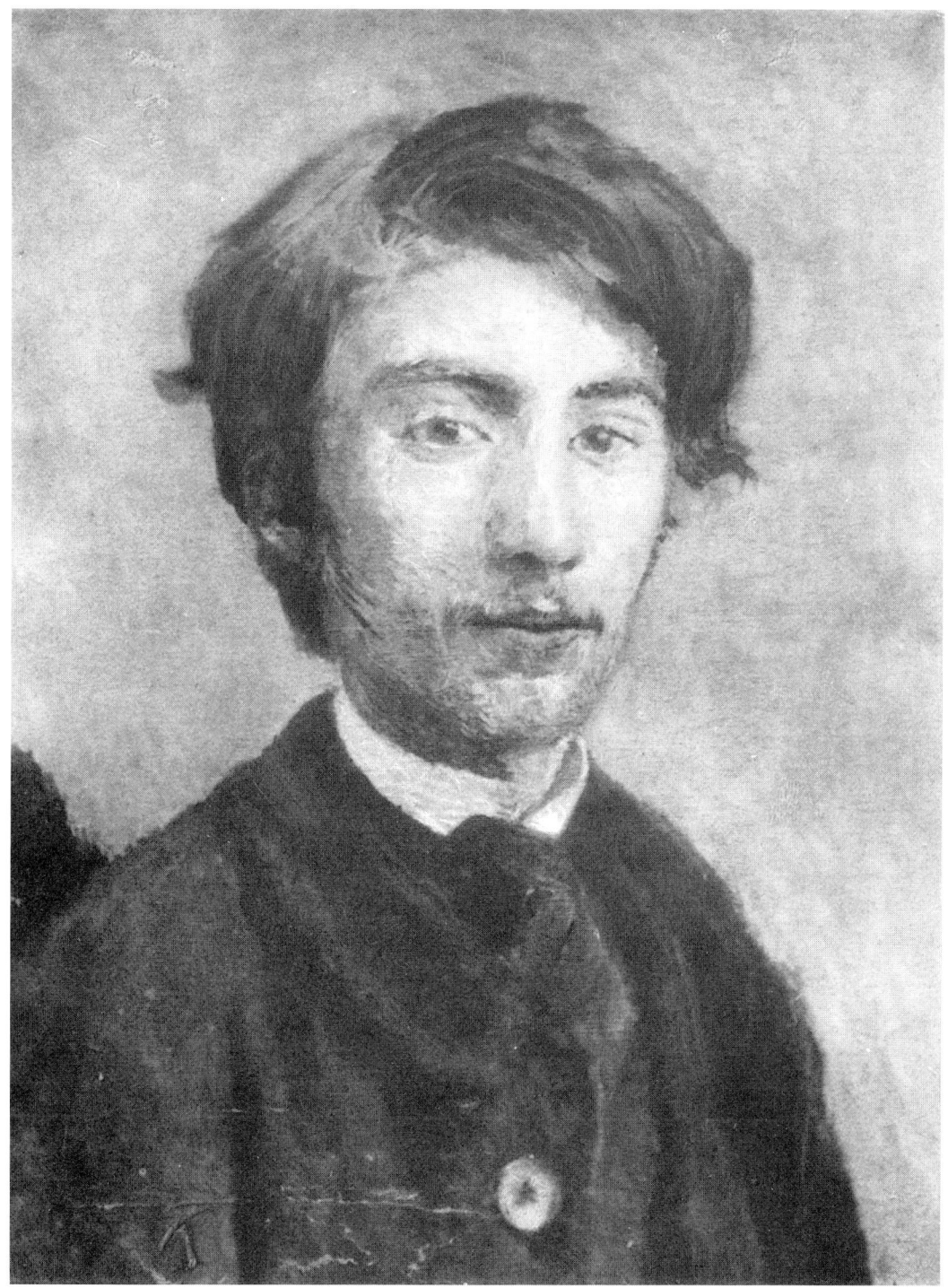

EMILE BERNARD BY HENRI DE TOULOUSE-LAUTREC

was at that time staying in the Pension Gloanec at Pont-Aven.[1] This man, an Alsatian, and former colleague of Gauguin when both were working in a bank in Paris, was Emile Schuffenecker, who had also given up business for painting and was now one of Gauguin's most intimate friends. Bernard accordingly went to Pont-Aven and introduced himself to Gauguin, but no friendship started between the two men. In 1888, after Gauguin's return from Martinique, they met there again and then, on the strength of a common interest in van Gogh, started that intimate acquaintance, a reflection of which can be seen through the letters in this volume, and which, as Mr. Robert Burnett says in his excellent biography of Gauguin, "was to drag on through many argumentative and acrimonious years a comedy of assertion and denial in the responsibility of who had, in fact, influenced whom".[2]

The story is a curious one indeed: Gauguin, one of the most affected, unpleasant and untruthful figures in the history of art, always denied that he had been influenced by Bernard. Actually there is no doubt from a study of the documents, both the present letters, the letters to Theo, the dates of Bernard's pictures and of those of Gauguin, that Gauguin stole ideas liberally from Bernard. But, being a more gifted painter, he worked them out more completely.

This was the period during which the School of Pont-Aven and the doctrine of Synthetism came to birth. In 1889, being denied space in the Palais des Beaux Arts at the Paris Exposition, the group organised their own exhibition at the Café Volpini, just outside the gates of the Exposition: they called themselves the *Groupe Impressioniste et Synthétiste*. Emile Bernard figured twice at this exhibition, for under the pseudonym of Ludovic Nemo, he exhibited a series of *peintures pétroles*, the colours being mixed with petrol instead of turpentine. Others of the group exhibiting were Gauguin, Charles Laval, Anquetin, Daniel de Monfried and Emile Schuffenecker. But much valuable and interesting information concerning the whole School of Pont-Aven and

[1] *Vide* LETTER II, note 3.

[2] *Paul Gauguin*, by Robert Burnett (Cobden-Sanderson, London, 1936), p. 63.

13

the doctrine of Synthetism remains hidden in the still unpublished correspondence between Emile Bernard and Gauguin.

In 1889 also, in a series entitled *Les Hommes d'Aujourd'hui*, Bernard published a laudatory article on Cézanne, whose work he knew purely from seeing it at the shop of Père Tanguy.[1] Bernard had never met Cézanne and in fact did not do so until 1904.

In 1891 Gauguin departed for the South Seas and with that the friendship ended. In 1893 Emile Bernard set out on a journey to Italy, Constantinople, Samos (where he painted some frescoes in a convent), Jerusalem, Tantah and Cairo. In Tantah he decorated a chapel: in Cairo he settled until 1904. Here he did a great deal of work including more frescoes in churches, but especially a series of large canvases about Arab life, one of which is now in the Lille Museum. Twice only did Bernard leave Cairo: once in 1896 on a long visit to Spain, and again in 1903 when he spent eight months in Venice.

In February 1904 he and his wife landed at Marseilles and immediately went to Aix en Provence to seek out his so-called *"premier maître d'élection"*, Paul Cézanne. According to his own account he was most cordially received. Bernard and his wife at once established themselves at Aix, where they remained for a month, seeing Cézanne almost daily. As Bernard says "The *bonhomie* in the character of Cézanne, who at once treated me like a colleague, despite our great difference in age, resulted in the growth of a strong bond between us". Actually Cézanne even placed one of the rooms of his studio on the Chemin des Lauves at the disposal of his young friend: the two painters also went off together to paint and had endless discussions about art. When Bernard finally departed for Paris they carried on a regular correspondence until Cézanne's death. They met for the second and last time at the beginning of 1905 when Bernard stopped at Aix on his way back from a visit to Naples.

But Bernard had succumbed too completely to the influence of the Old Masters, particularly the Venetian School, to profit fully by Cézanne's advice. Thus on 13th September, 1906, we find Cézanne writing to his son: "I am sending you a letter which I have received

[1] *Vide* LETTER XIV, note 10.

from Emilio Bernardinos, the most distinguished æsthete, whom I regret not to have under my thumb in order to suggest to him the idea, so wholesome, so helpful and so right of a development of art in contact with nature . . . The good fellow turns his back completely on what he maintains in his writings, in his work he does only old-fashioned things, which show the influence of his ideas of art suggested not by the emotions of nature, but by what he has been able to see in museums, and still more by a philosophic spirit, which comes from a too great knowledge of the masters he admires."[1]

Bernard's work is obsessed with a return to Classicism. He founded a society called the *Rénovation Esthétique*, which lasted only five years: he gave lectures and wrote two books on the subject—'*L'Esthétique Fondamentale*' and '*Sur l'art et sur les Maîtres*'. He also wrote for various reviews such as the *Gazette des Beaux Arts* and *Mercure de France*; the latter published three admirable articles by him on Cézanne in the editions of 1st and 15th October 1907, 1st March 1920 and 1st June 1921.

He has also written a great deal in favour of van Gogh. It is probably to Emile Bernard more than to anyone else that the early recognition of van Gogh is due. He wrote very many articles about his work and was largely responsible for the organisation of the first exhibition in Paris in 1892.

Since 1922 he has lived a great deal in Italy, mostly in Venice. He has published a large volume on Michelangelo and in 1925 a volume '*Sur Cézanne*'. There are frequent references to his poetry in the ensuing letters, though naturally only to his earliest efforts. He has subsequently written a great deal more, some of which has been published under the pseudonym of Jean d'Orsal.

Add to all this his carved furniture, tapestries, book-illustrations, sculptures, engravings on wood and other materials, campaigns for the preservation of old churches as well as of the Ile St. Louis, in the middle of the Seine directly behind Nôtre-Dame, where he lives today, and one has a complete picture of the man and his activities.

[1] I quote this translation from *Paul Cézanne*, by Gerstle Mack, p. 383; for the original text *vide Paul Cézanne: Correspondence*, edited by John Rewald (Grasset, Paris, 1938).

15

LETTERS TO EMILE BERNARD
I—XXIII

Dear old Bernard,[2]

I feel I owe you an apology for having left you so abruptly the other day. So I do this here without delay. I recommend you to read Tolstoy's russian legends,[3] and I will also get for you the article on Eug[ène] Delacroix which I spoke about.

Personally I went to see Guillaumin[4] all the same, but in the evening: and it occurred to me that perhaps you do not know his address, which is: 13 Quai d'Anjou. As a man, I think Guillaumin is more sure of his ideas than the others, and if all were like him they would produce more good work and have less time or desire to snap at each other.

I persist in believing that you will one day realise, not because I have rammed it down your throat, but because with you too it will become a conviction, I believe that in time you will come to realise that in the studios one not only does not learn much about painting, but not even much in the way of a technique of life: so one is obliged to learn how to live, as well as how to paint, without having recourse to the old tricks and optical illusions of intriguers.[5]

I do not think your self-portrait will be either your last or your best, although as a matter of fact it is terribly you.

Listen now, what I was trying to explain to you the other day amounts roughly to this. In order to avoid generalisations allow me to take an actual example. If you have quarrelled with a painter and as a result you say: "If Signac[6] exhibits in the place where I exhibit, I shall remove my pictures," and if you abuse him, then it seems to me that you are not behaving as well as you might.

For it is better to look at things for a long while and make sure before judging them categorically; reflection often shows us in the case of quarrels, that one side is as much wrong as the other—and that one's adversary has as much justification as one would claim for oneself.

If then you have already decided that Signac and the others who use pointillism quite often produce very beautiful works, instead of disparaging these you must, if you have quarrelled, above all esteem them and talk sympathetically of them.

Otherwise one becomes sectarian, narrow-minded and like those people who have no use for anyone else, believing themselves only to be right.

This applies even to the academicians: take for example a picture by Fantin-Latour,[7] or rather the whole of his work. Well, there's someone who's no revolutionary; but that does not prevent his having that sort of calm and correctness which makes him one of the most independent characters alive.

One more word about the military service which you will be obliged to do.[8] You must concern yourself with that right away. Directly by finding out exactly what can be arranged in such cases to enable you first of all to keep the right to work, to choose your garrison, etc.: but indirectly by taking care of your health. You must not begin in too nervous or anæmic a condition if you really wish to come out of it stronger.

I do not consider it a great misfortune for you that you are bound to go off and be a soldier, but rather a grave trial out of which—if you come through—you will emerge a very great artist.

Do all you can between now and then to get strong, for you will need plenty of vigour. And if you work a lot during that year, I think you might end by having a good stock of pictures, some of which we will try to sell for you, as you will be in need of pocket-money to pay for models.

I will of course do all I can to make a success of what we have begun in the café[9]; but I am afraid the first condition of success is to forget our petty jealousies, only union makes strength. In the common interest it is worth while abandoning the egotistic doctrine: each one for himself.

A hearty handshake,
Vincent.

¹ I suggest this vague date because it accords with the date given to *Letters to Theo* Nos. 460–2, in which the Café Tambourin affair is obviously over. *Vide* note 9. This letter is written on plain white paper measuring 8 × 5¼ inches (20.5 × 13.2 cm.).

² I have throughout translated thus the phrase *Mon cher copain Bernard*; the expression "My dear pal" seeming to me impossible, although more accurate.

³ He writes "*légendes russes*," without capital letters. This probably means his collections of russian tales.

⁴ Armand Guillaumin (1841–1927), a member of the Impressionist group and friend of Pissarro.

⁵ "*aux vieux trucs et trompe-l'oeil d'intrigants . . .*"

⁶ Paul Signac (1863–1935), a friend of Seurat and with him the chief exponent of Pointillism, the technique of producing luminosity by covering the surface of the canvas with little dots of the prismatic colours which are then blended by the eye.

⁷ Henri-Jean-Ignace-Théodore Fantin-Latour (1836–1904), a friend of the Impressionist painters, though not a member of the group, famous for his very naturalistic paintings of flowers and fruit, as well as for his large group portraits of artists, musicians, poets.

⁸ Vincent was much concerned about Bernard's military service as these letters all show. Actually, owing to ill-health, Bernard never did his service, being finally placed in the Service Auxiliaire and never called up.

⁹ The café referred to is the Café Tambourin in the Avenue de Clichy, owned by an artists' model, Agostina Segatori. Vincent, having made friends with the *patronne*, arranged for the exhibition there of pictures by himself, Anquetin, Lautrec and Bernard. He also painted some decorations for the café, which, it seems (*vide Letters to Theo* Nos. 461 and 462) they refused to give back to him when the concern went bankrupt. Emile Bernard adds that, as far as the exhibition was concerned, Vincent, having had a row with the *patronne*, arrived one day with a hand-cart and removed all the pictures to his studio in the Rue Lepic.

My dear Bernard,

Having promised to write to you I want to begin by telling you that this countryside seems to me as beautiful as Japan for clarity of atmosphere and gay colour effects. Water forms patches of lovely emerald or rich blue in the landscape, just as we see it in the crape-prints.[2] The pale orange of the sunsets makes the fields appear blue. The sun is a splendid yellow. However, I have still not really seen the countryside in all its habitual summer splendour. The women's costume is pretty, and on Sundays especially, one sees on the boulevards some naïve and very happy combinations of colours. And in summer, no doubt, they will become even more gay.

The trouble is that life here is not as cheap as I had hoped, and I have not yet found the way to manage as well as one would at Pont-Aven.[3] I began by paying 5 francs, and am now down to 4 francs a day. One should really speak the local *patois* and get to like *bouilla-baisse*[4] and *aïoli*, then one would be certain to find a cheap middle-class pension. Then, if there were several of us one would, I am convinced, obtain better terms still. There might even be a material advantage for several of those artists who love the sun and bright colours to move to the south.

Even if the Japanese are not developing in their own country, it is certain that their art is finding its development in France. At the head of this letter you will find a rough sketch of a subject of which I hope to make something[5]: sailors returning with their sweethearts to the town, whose strange drawbridge stands out in silhouette against an enormous yellow sun. I have another version of the same subject with a group of washerwomen.[6]

Shall be happy to have a word from you telling what you are doing and where you are going.

A hearty handshake for yourself and our friends.

Ever yours,

Vincent.

PLATE 3

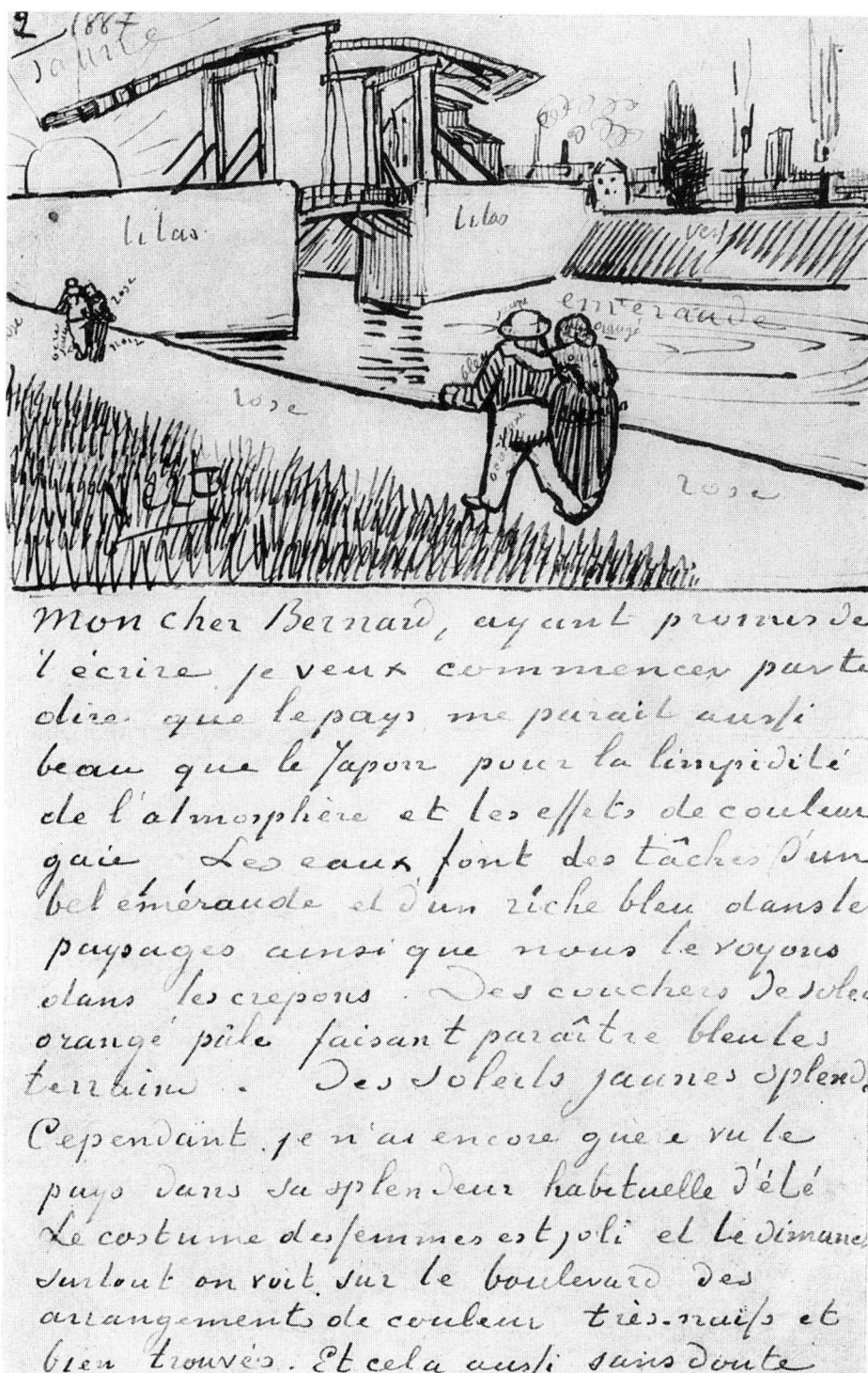

FACSIMILE FROM LETTER II

PLATE 4

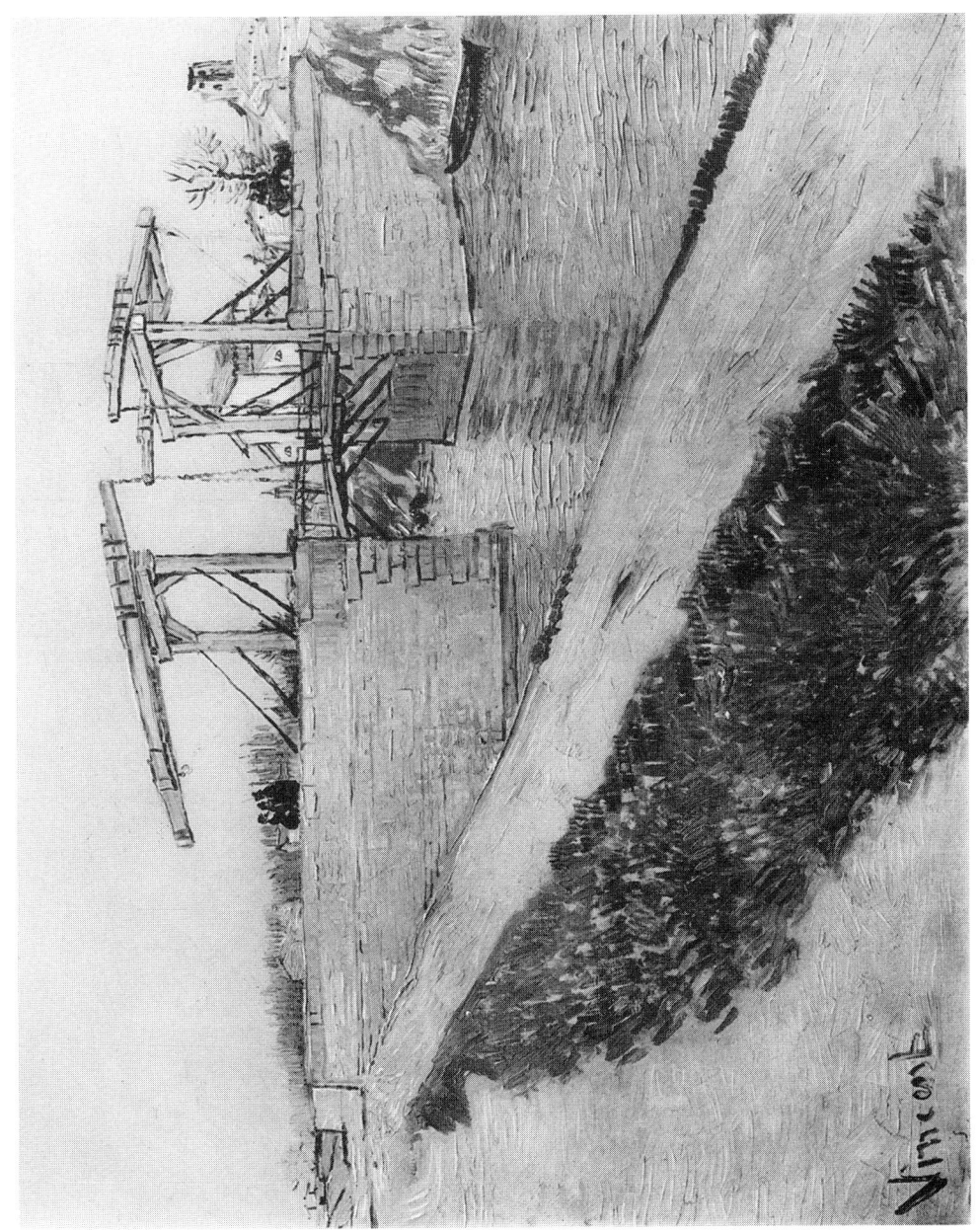

THE DRAWBRIDGE NEAR ARLES

¹ *Vide Letters to Theo* Nos. 469, 470, 471, which relate to the drawing at the head of this letter. This letter is written on plain white paper measuring $7\frac{7}{8} \times 5\frac{1}{8}$ inches (20 × 13 cm.) and is obviously the one enclosed with one for Lautrec in Letter 470.

² *"crépons"*: Vincent must be referring to Japanese pictures printed on crape-silk, or on cotton or on paper. The word is uncommon.

³ A small town in Brittany, near Lorient in the Finistère district. There was a colony of painters there and the cost of living was notoriously low. It was much frequented by Gauguin, who was there for over six months in 1886, and again in 1888: other painters included Emile Bernard, Schuffenecker, Charles Laval and Sérusier. They all stayed at a *pension* near the bridge over the River Aven, owned by a Madame Gloanec, who charged about 60 to 70 francs a month, i.e. £2 to £3. The academic painters who stayed there hated the group of advanced painters and referred to them as the Succursale de Charenton, Charenton being the largest and best-known lunatic asylum in France. Pont-Aven was the birthplace of the theory of Synthetism. "Synthetism was nothing more than an intentional simplification of lines, forms and colours, a simplification having as its objective to give to expression a maximum of intensity through the suppression of everything that could lessen the effect. This method of interpretation was not, to tell the truth, a discovery, for, since the origins of painting, this simplification is the actual basis of decorative art . . ." I quote this translation of de Rotonchamps' (one of the members of the new group) definition from Mr. Robert Burnett's *Life of Paul Gauguin* (Cobden-Sanderson, London, 1936).

⁴ A Provençal dish composed of fish, lobsters, mussels, etc., cooked in white wine and flavoured with garlic, parsley, saffron, pepper, bay leaves, etc. *Aïoli* is another Provençal dish, the basis of which is chopped garlic.

⁵ *Vide* Plates 3 and 4. If he ever did do a picture it has now vanished: but the group of two figures in the foreground is the subject of de la Faille No. 544.

⁶ de la Faille No. 397 or 571.

III

Dear old Bernard,

Thank you for your nice letter and the enclosed sketches of your decoration, which I find very amusing. I regret sometimes that I can't make up my mind to work more at home and from memory. The imagination is certainly a faculty which we must develop and it alone can bring us to the creation of a more exalting and consoling nature than we are shown in a solitary glance at reality—which we perceive as changing, flashing by like lightning.

A star-spangled sky for example, that's a thing I would like to try and do,[2] just as by daylight I shall attempt to paint a green meadow spangled with dandelions.[3] But how can I manage unless I make up my mind to work at home and from imagination? That's a criticism of me, and a credit to you.

At the moment, I am busy with blossoming fruit trees; pink peach blossom, white and yellow pear blossom.[4] I don't keep to any one technique. I dab the colour irregularly on the canvas and leave it at that. Here lumps of thick paint, there bits of canvas left uncovered, elsewhere portions left quite unfinished, new beginnings, coarsenesses: but anyway the result, it seems to me, is alarming and provocative enough to disturb those people who have fixed preconceived ideas about technique. Here, by the way, is a sketch, the entrance to a Provençal orchard with its yellow fence, its screen of black cypresses (against the mistral), its characteristic vegetables of varying greens: yellow salad vegetables, onions, garlic, emerald-green leeks.[5]

While working directly on the spot all the time, I try to secure the essential in the drawing—then I go for the spaces, bounded by contours, either expressed or not, but felt at all events: these I fill with tones equally simplified, so that all that is going to be soil partakes of the same purplish tone, the whole of the sky has a blueish hue and the greens are either definitely blue-greens or yellow-greens, purposely exaggerating in this case the yellow or blue qualities.

Anyway, my dear old friend, there's no attempt at perspective.

As regards my idea of visiting Aix, Marseilles and Tangier, there's

PLATE 5

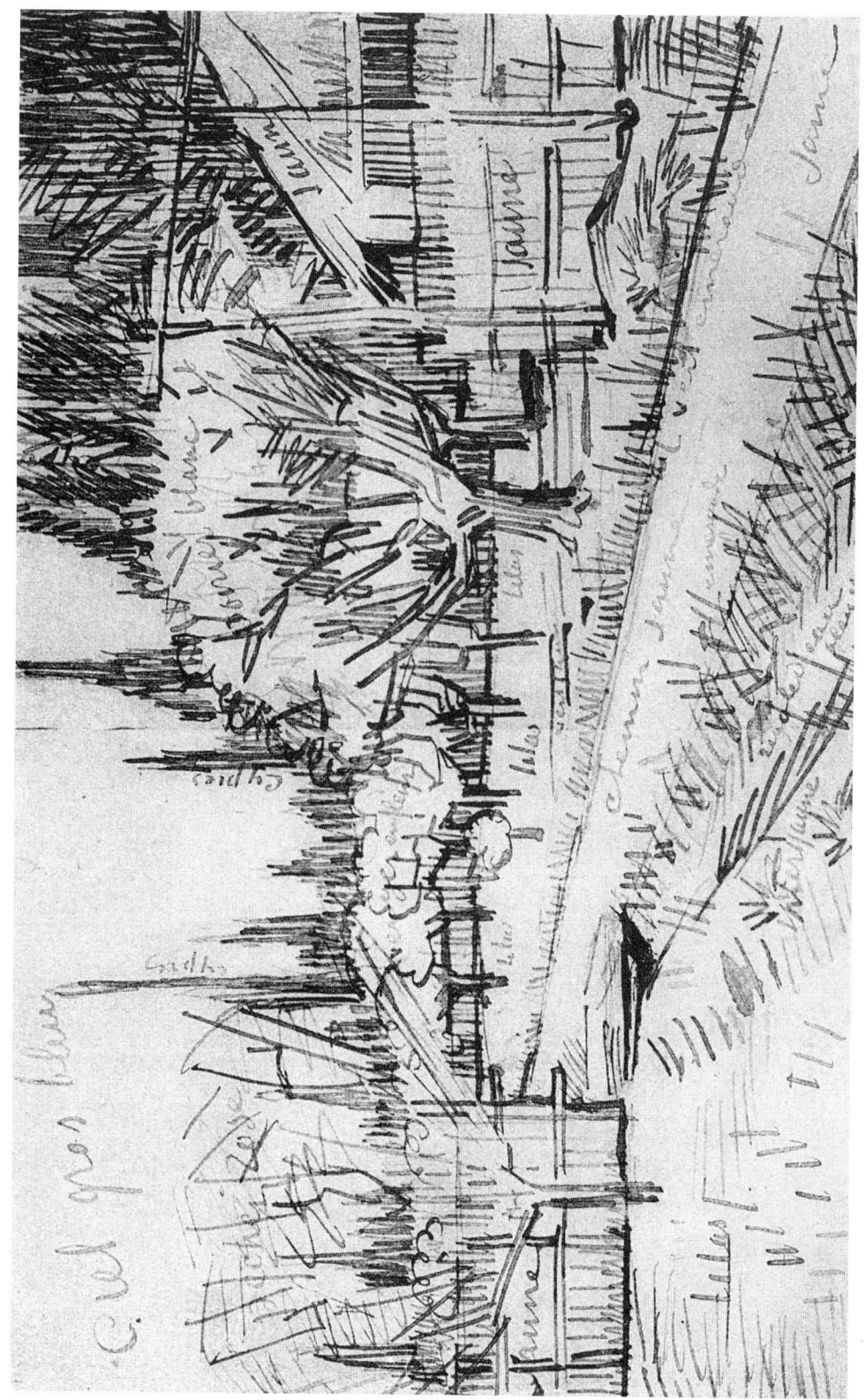

FACSIMILE FROM LETTER III

PLATE 6

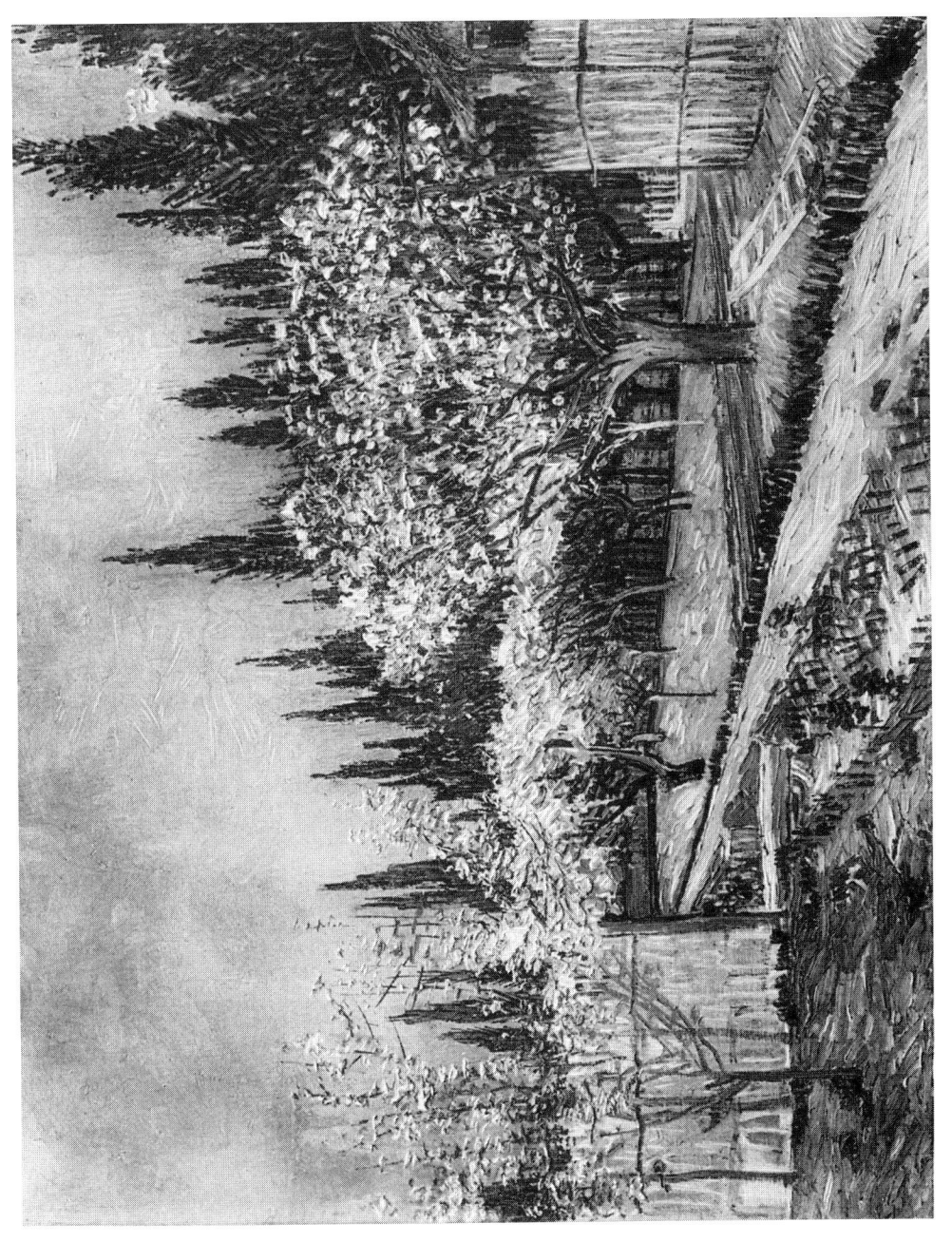

A PROVENÇAL ORCHARD

no danger at present. If by any chance I do go it will be in search of cheaper lodging. Otherwise I realise only too clearly that even were I to work here the whole of my life I could scarcely record half of what is characteristic of this town alone.

By the way, I have seen some bull-fights in the arena,[6] or rather they were sham fights, considering that the bulls were numerous, and no one fought them. But the crowd was magnificent, a huge multi-coloured mass piled up through two or three tiers of seats, with the effects of sun and shade and the shadow cast by the enormous ring.

I wish you a good journey[7]—a handshake in thought,

Your friend,

Vincent.

[1] *Vide Letters to Theo* Nos. 471–474: *vide* also *A Note on the Orchards in Bloom* by Drs. Scherjon and Gruyter in their *Catalogue of van Gogh's Great Period, Arles-Auvers.* This letter is written on plain white paper measuring $8 \times 5\frac{1}{4}$ inches (20.5 × 13.2 cm.). The drawing of the orchard is on a separate sheet of the same size.

[2] Such a picture exists: de la Faille No. 474.

[3] Drs. Scherjon and Gruyter suggest that this is de la Faille No. 575, not perhaps with much justification.

[4] de la Faille Nos. 404, 555, 403, 405, 556 are probably those referred to.

[5] *Vide* Plates 5 and 6. The finished picture is de la Faille No. 554: a second version is de la Faille No. 513.

[6] This is the subject of de la Faille No. 548; these would be the bull-fights mentioned in Letter 474 to Theo.

[7] Bernard was again setting out on his annual walking excursion in Brittany to paint. See *A Note on Emile Bernard* in the present volume.

Dear old Bernard,

Many thanks for the sonnets you sent me, I like both the form and the music of the first enormously:

Sous les dômes dormeurs des arbres gigantesques.[2]

But for idea and sentiment, it is perhaps the last one which I prefer:

Car l'espoir dans mon sein a versé sa névrose.[3]

But I don't think you express clearly enough what it is you want us to feel: the certainty which one seems to have, and which one can, in any case, prove, of the nothingness, the emptiness, the treachery of the good or beautiful things one desires; and how, despite this knowledge, we allow ourselves to be eternally deceived by the charm cast over our 6 senses by the external world, by things outside ourselves, as though we understood nothing, and especially not the difference between objectivity and subjectivity. Luckily for us, we remain in this way both stupid and full of hope.

But I like too:

L'hiver, n'avoir ni sou, ni fleurs,[4]

and *Mépris.*

Coin de Chapelle and *Dessin d'Albert Dürer*, I find less clear: which, for example, is the drawing of Albert Dürer exactly? But there are nevertheless excellent passages in it:

Venus des plaines bleues
Blêmis par la longueur des lieues[5]

is an awfully good description of the landscapes bristling with blue rocks and the roads winding their way between them, as in the backgrounds of Cranach and van Eyck.

Tordu sur sa croix en spirale[6]

conveys very well the exaggerated leanness of many a mystic Christ. But why not add that the anguished look of the martyr has some of the same despair which one sees in the eye of a cab-horse; this would make it more truly Parisian, for there one sees that sort of look both

PLATE 7

FACSIMILE FROM LETTER IV

PLATE 8

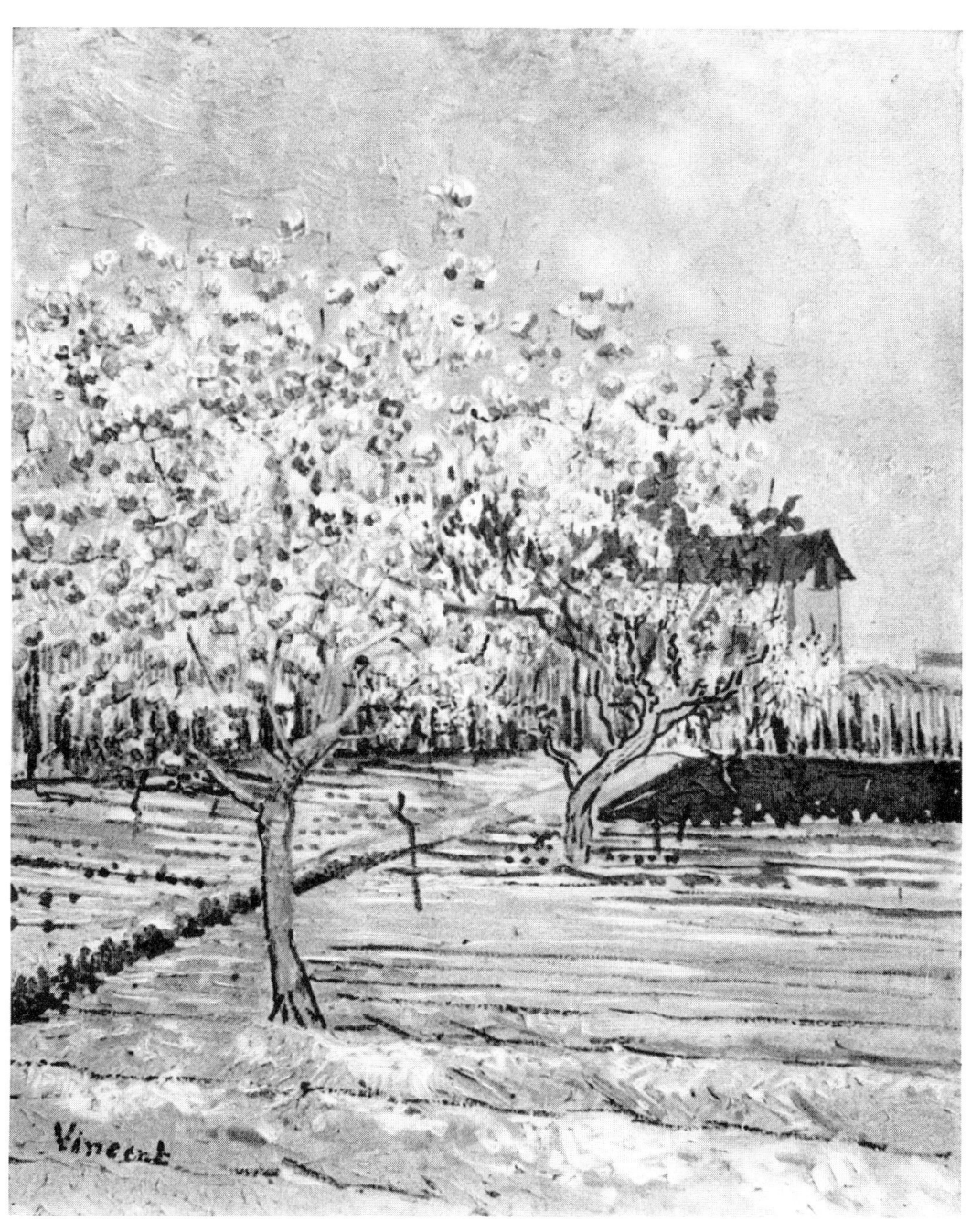

A PROVENÇAL ORCHARD

in the eyes of invalids in their chairs and in those of poets or artists.

In short it's not yet as good as your painting: but that doesn't matter, it will be in time—you must certainly continue your sonnets. There are so many people, especially among our pals, who imagine that words are nothing: but, on the contrary, it's as interesting and as difficult to say a thing well as to paint it, isn't it? There is the art of lines and colours, but the art of words exists too, and will never be less important.

Here's a fresh orchard, simple enough as a composition: a white tree, a small green tree, a square patch of green, lilac soil, an orange roof, a big blue sky.[7]

I have nine orchards on hand:[8] one white, one pink almost red, one bluish white, one pinkish grey, one green and pink.

I worked one [canvas] to death yesterday, a cherry tree against a blue sky, the young leaf-shoots were gold and orange, the clusters of flowers white, and that against the green-blue of the sky made a glorious show. Today alas there's rain, which prevents my going to have another shot at it.

I saw a brothel here on Sunday—not counting the other days— a spacious room, whitewashed but with a bluish tinge—like a village school. Fifty or more military men in red and civilians in black, their faces a splendid yellow or orange (there's such colour in the faces here!), the women in sky-blue, in vermillion, everything that's most pure and most garish. The whole in a yellow light. A good deal less dismal than similar institutions in Paris.

Depression isn't in the air down here.

At the moment, I am still being very good and keeping quiet, as I must first of all deal with that stomach trouble whose happy victim I am: after that I shall have a grand time, for I aspire to share some of the immortality of the great Tartarin de Tarascon.[9]

I was very interested to hear that you intend spending your military service in Algeria. It's perfect, and jolly far from being a misfortune. I congratulate you really; anyway we will meet in Marseilles.

You'll see then how happy it'll make you to see the blue here, and to feel the sun.

I have a balcony now for studio.

I certainly mean to go and paint the sea around Marseilles, I don't at all long for the grey North Sea. If you see Gauguin, greet him kindly from me. I have to write to him just now.

Don't despair my dear Bernard, and above all don't get depressed old man, because with your talent, your stay in Algeria will make a thoroughly good, real artist of you. You too will become a southerner. If I have any advice to give you it is to fortify yourself: *yes*, eat sensibly for at least a year in advance. Start now in fact, because it's no good arriving here with your stomach out of order and your blood in a poor state.

That's the condition I was in and although I'm on the mend now, the process is slow and I regret not having been a bit more careful beforehand. But in such a damnable winter as the last, there was nothing to be done, it was unnatural.

Get your blood in good condition then beforehand: it's difficult to do anything about it here, with the bad food, but once one is well it's less difficult than in Paris to remain so.

Write to me soon, always the same address: Restaurant Carrel,[10] Arles.

A handshake,
Yours,
Vincent.

[1] In *Letters to Theo* No. 477 he mentions the receipt of Bernard's sonnets; Letter 478 is dated 20th April and contains a drawing of the same subject. This letter is written on plain white paper measuring $8 \times 5\frac{1}{4}$ inches (20.5 × 13.2 cm.).

[2] "Beneath the dreaming domes of the gigantic trees . . ."

[3] "For hope has poured its neurosis into my bosom . . ."

[4] "In winter, having neither money nor flowers . . ."

[5] "Arrivals from the blue plains, pallid from the endless leagues . . ."

[6] "Writhing on his Cross in spirals . . ."

[7] *Vide* Plates 7 and 8. A drawing of the same subject is included in *Letters to Theo* No. 478. The finished picture is de la Faille No. 406.

[8] *Vide Letters to Theo* No. 477: "That will make 6 canvases of orchards in bloom . . . I dare to hope for three more, matching in the same way . . . I would so like to do this series of 9 canvases . . ."; also *Van Gogh and John Russell; an unpublished correspondence* by Henry Thannhauser, Letter I, *Burlington Magazine*, September 1938: "I am working at a series of blooming orchards."

[9] Hero of three satirical novels of Provence, '*Tartarin de Tarascon*', '*Tartarin sur les Alpes*' and '*Port-Tarascon*' by Alphonse Daudet (1840–97). Tartarin is now a national figure: the boasting, but outspoken Southerner.

[10] Near the station in the Rue Cavalerie.

V

My dear Bernard,

I have just received your last letter. You are quite right to see that these negresses were heart-rending; and quite right too not to believe it was innocent.[2]

I have just read a book—not good and not well written either—about the Marquesas Islands, but very moving in its account of the extermination of a whole native tribe, admittedly a man-eating tribe inasmuch as let us say about once a month somebody got eaten—and what's that?

So the whites, true Christians, etc. . . . in order to put an end to such barbarianism (?) *which was really very mild,* could find no better way than to wipe out both the man-eating natives and the tribe with which they used to fight the battles (which were calculated to provide both sides with the necessary prisoners to be eaten).

Then they annexed the two Isles, and now what gloom!

These tattooed tribes, negroes, Indians, all of them are either disappearing or degenerating. And the dreadful white man with his bottle of alcohol, his money and his pox—when will they have seen enough of him? The dreadful white man: hypocritical, greedy, sterile.

And those savages were so gentle, so loving.

You are quite right to think of Gauguin. There's great poetry in his pictures of negresses: everything he does has something gentle, heart-rending, astonishing. People don't understand him yet; and he's very upset he doesn't sell, like other real poets.

I would have written to you before old man, only I had several things on hand. First of all I've sent off a first batch of studies to my brother.[3]

Secondly I've been having trouble with my health.

Thirdly I've rented a house, painted yellow outside, whitewashed within and standing full in the sun (four rooms).[4]

On top of that I've started some new studies. And in the evening I was often too worn out to write. That's why my answer has been delayed.

PLATE 9

VAN GOGH'S HOUSE AT ARLES

Your sonnet about the women of the streets has some good stuff in it: but it does not quite come off, the ending is banal. A *"sublime woman..."* I don't know what you mean by that: and nor do you in this case.

Then there's

> *Dans le clan des vieux et des jeunes maraude*
> *Ceux qu'elle emmènera coucher le soir, très tard.*[5]

[or] something like that, it's not characteristic at all, for the women of our boulevard—the little one—usually sleep *alone* at night, as they have five or six customers during the day or in the evening and *très tard* it's that carnivorous worthy their *maquereau*[6] who comes and fetches them home, but they don't sleep together (except occasionally). A woman who's worn out usually goes to bed alone and sleeps like a log.[7]

But if you change 2 or 3 lines it'll be all right.

What have you been painting recently? As to me I've done a still life with a blue enamelled iron coffee pot,[8] a royal blue cup and saucer, a milk jug checkered pale cobalt and white, a cup with a pattern in blue and orange on a white ground, a blue majolica jug decorated with flowers and foliage in greens, browns and pinks. All that on a blue tablecloth, against a yellow background; there are also two oranges and three lemons among this crockery.

So it's a variety of blues livened up by a whole range of yellows, running even into orange.

Then I have another still life: lemons in a basket against a yellow background.[9]

Then a view of Arles.[10] Of the town itself only a few red roofs and a tower are visible, the rest is hidden behind the green foliage of fig-trees away in the background: a narrow strip of blue sky is above. The town is surrounded by huge meadows abounding in buttercups —a sea of yellow: right in the foreground a ditch filled with violet irises cuts through these meadows. The grass was cut whilst I was painting, so that it's only a study and not the finished picture I had the intention of making. But what a subject, eh? That sea of gold with a band of purple irises, and in the background the enchanting little town with its pretty women! Then two studies beside main roads —later—done with the *mistral* raging.

If you weren't so anxious for my answer I would make you rough sketches.

Keep your courage up: good luck. A handshake. I am worn out tonight. I'll write again in the next few days when I have more time.

Vincent.

PS. The portrait of a woman, in your last letter but one,[11] is very nice. My address: 2, Place Lamartine, Arles.

[1] *Vide Letters to Theo* No. 489 which contains a drawing of the STILL LIFE WITH A BLUE ENAMEL COFFEE POT. This letter is written on plain white paper measuring $8 \times 5\frac{1}{4}$ inches (20.5×13.2 cm.).

[2] This refers to a picture which Gauguin had brought back from Martinique and which Bernard had seen at Theo van Gogh's gallery.

[3] *Vide Letters to Theo* No. 483.

[4] Plate 9. The so-called Yellow House in the Place Lamartine (de la Faille No. 464); *vide* also *Letters to Theo* No. 480 with rough sketch.

[5] "Eyeing among the groups of old and young, those whom she will take to bed with her that night, very late . . ."

[6] Pimp, pander.

PLATE 10

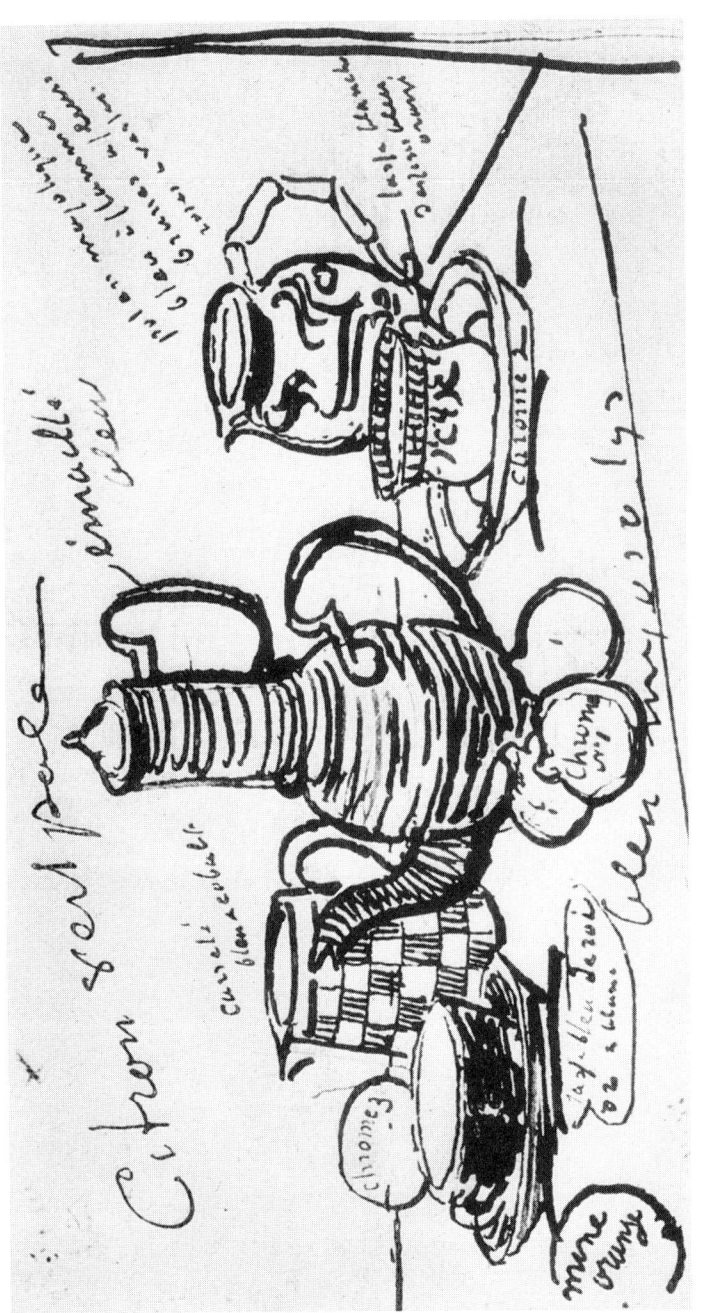

FACSIMILE FROM LETTER VI

PLATE 11

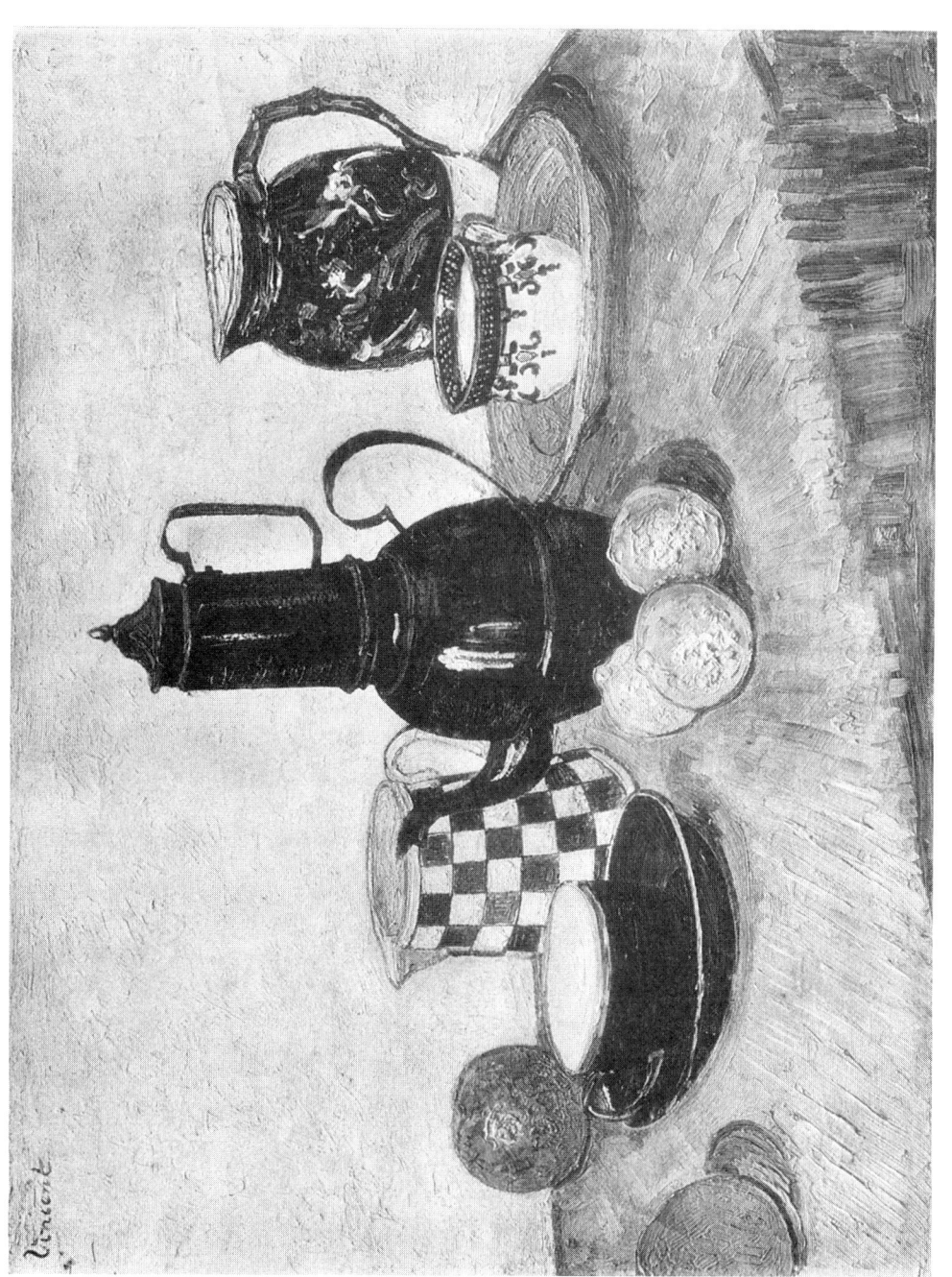

STILL LIFE WITH COFFEE-POT

[7] The poem of Bernard's here referred to, written in October 1887, is as follows:

La Prostitution
A Vincent

La Prostitution sort couverte de fard
Le long du boulevard lumineux elle rôde
Et dans le clan des vieux et des jeunes maraude
Ceux qu'elle emmènera coucher ce soir, très tard.

Certes, si sa beauté n'est exquise, comme Aude
Elle n'en est pas moins très séduisante, car
Qu'importe la beauté si son ivresse est chaude
Et connaît cet amour dont elle-même est l'art!

Allons tous deux, ami, vers sa funèbre orgie;
J'aime sa nudité flambant sous la bougie;
Allons pour lui ravir ses bas et son corset.

Et quand sur nos genoux nous l'aurons mise nue,
Que le fard tombera, quelque femme inconnue
Surgira, qui sera plus sublime . . . qui sait?

[8] de la Faille No. 410: *vide* Plates 10 and 11.

[9] de la Faille No. 384.

[10] de la Faille No. 409; *vide* also *Letters to Theo* No. 487, which contains a similar drawing.

[11] This would refer to a letter with sketches written about 1st May and mentioned as having been received in *Letters to Theo* No. 480.

33

VI

Dear old Bernard,

More and more it seems to me that the pictures which must be painted to make present-day painting completely itself and raise it to a height equal to the serene peaks which were attained by the Greek sculptors, the German musicians, and the French novelists, are beyond the power of one isolated individual. They will therefore probably be created by groups of men combining together to execute an idea held in common.

One person may have a superb control of colour, and be lacking in ideas.

Another bubbling over with new, heartrending or charming conceptions, but, because of a timid limited palette, quite unable to express them sonorously enough.

This is the great reason for regretting the lack of communal feeling among artists, who criticise and persecute each other without, happily, ever being able to annihilate one another.

You will perhaps say that all this reasoning is banal—so it may be. But there is the thing itself: the existence of a Renaissance, and this fact indeed is not a banality.

Now for a technical question. Give me some of your views in your next letter.

It's about *black* and *white*; I am going to put them brazenly on my palette just as I get them from the colour merchant, and use them like that. When—remember I am talking about simplification of colour in the Japanese style—when in a green park, with pink paths, I see a man dressed in black, a justice of the peace by profession (the arabian Jew in Daudet's '*Tartarin*' calls this honourable functionary a *zouge de paix*²) reading *L'Intransigeant*,³ and above him and the park a pure cobalt sky: then why not paint the said *zouge de paix* in pure black and *L'Intransigeant* in pure unadulterated white?

For the Japanese make an abstraction of reflections, placing flat tones next to one another, with characteristic lines defining the movements or forms.

PLATE 12

FACSIMILE FROM LETTER VI

In another category of ideas, when one composes a colour *motif* expressive, for example, of a yellow evening sky, the hard unadulterated whiteness of a white wall against the sky can if necessary be brought out in a curious way by flattening out the pure white with some neutral tone, for the sky itself gives it a pale lilac hue. Imagine as well in this simple but imaginary landscape, a cottage, whitewashed all over (including the roof), the surrounding soil being orange-coloured, naturally, for the southern sun and the blueness of the Mediterranean produce an orange which increases in intensity in proportion to the brilliance of the scale of blues, then the black note of the door, the windows and the little crucifix on top of the roof produce an immediate contrast of black and white as satisfying to the eye as that of the blue and orange.[4]

Or, to take a more amusing example, let us imagine a woman in a black and white check dress placed in this same elementary landscape with its blue sky and orange soil; it would be a fairly curious sight, I imagine. At Arles actually they wear much black and white check.

Suffice it that black and white too are colours, for in many cases they can be treated as colours, their immediate contrast being as violent as, for example, that of red and green.

As a matter of fact, the Japanese make use of it. They express marvellously well the contrast between the dull pale complexion of some girl and the vivid blackness of her hair, with nothing but a sheet of white paper and four strokes of the pen. Not to mention their spikey black bushes dotted with a thousand little white flowers.

At last I have seen the Mediterranean, which, probably, you will cross before I do. I have spent a week at Saintes-Maries,[5] and to get there drove in a *diligence* across the Camargue with its vineyards, moors, flat stretches of land as in Holland. There, at Saintes-Maries, there were some girls reminiscent of Cimabue or Giotto, slender, erect, a little sad and mystic. On the beach, quite flat and sandy, there are little boats, green, red and blue, so pretty in form and colour that one is reminded of flowers.[6] One man alone can manage them, they don't venture far out. When there is no wind they're off, but back they come if there's even a little too much.[7]

Gauguin it seems is still ill.

I am wondering what you have been working at lately: myself I am still always working at landscapes, here's a sketch.[8] I should also love to take a look at Africa, but I hardly have any definite plans for the future, that depends on circumstances.

What I want to find out is the effect of a more intense blue in the sky. Fromentin[9] and Gérôme[10] find the southern landscape colourless, and lots of people see it that way. But, my God, if you take some sand in your hands and look at it closely, or study even water or air in that way, they will all seem colourless. *There's no blue without yellow and orange,* and if you put a blue you must put the yellow and the orange too, mustn't you? But you'll tell me I only write to you of banalities.

A handshake in thought.

Yours,

Vincent.

PLATE 13

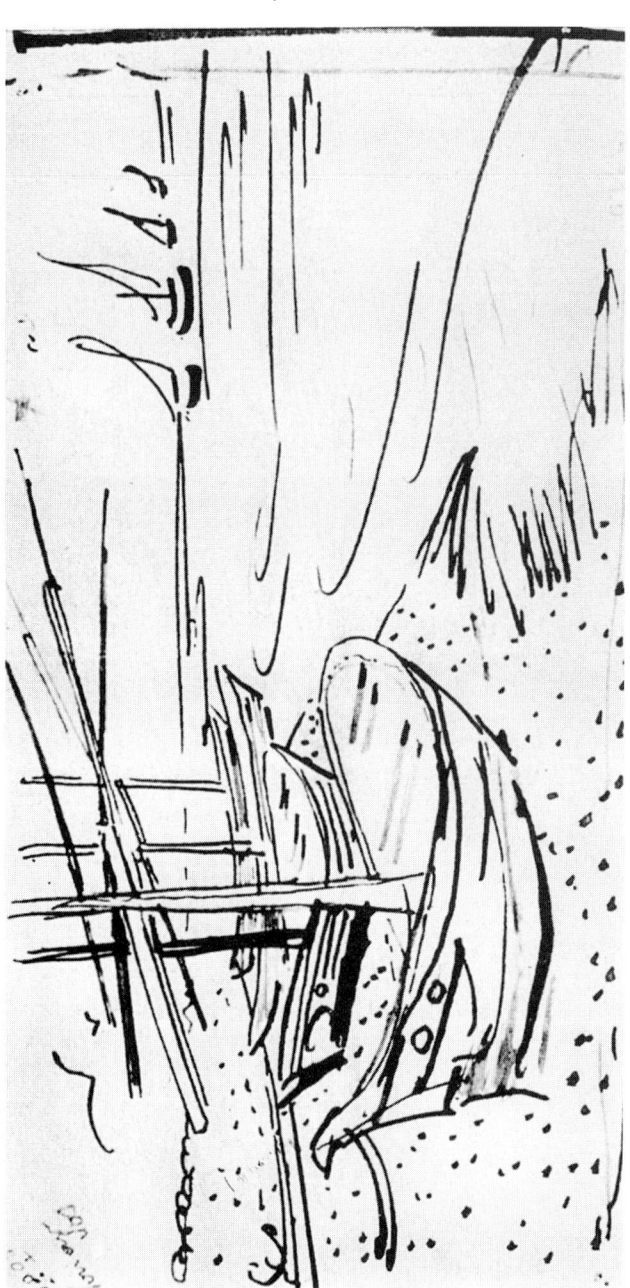

FACSIMILE FROM LETTER VI

PLATE 14

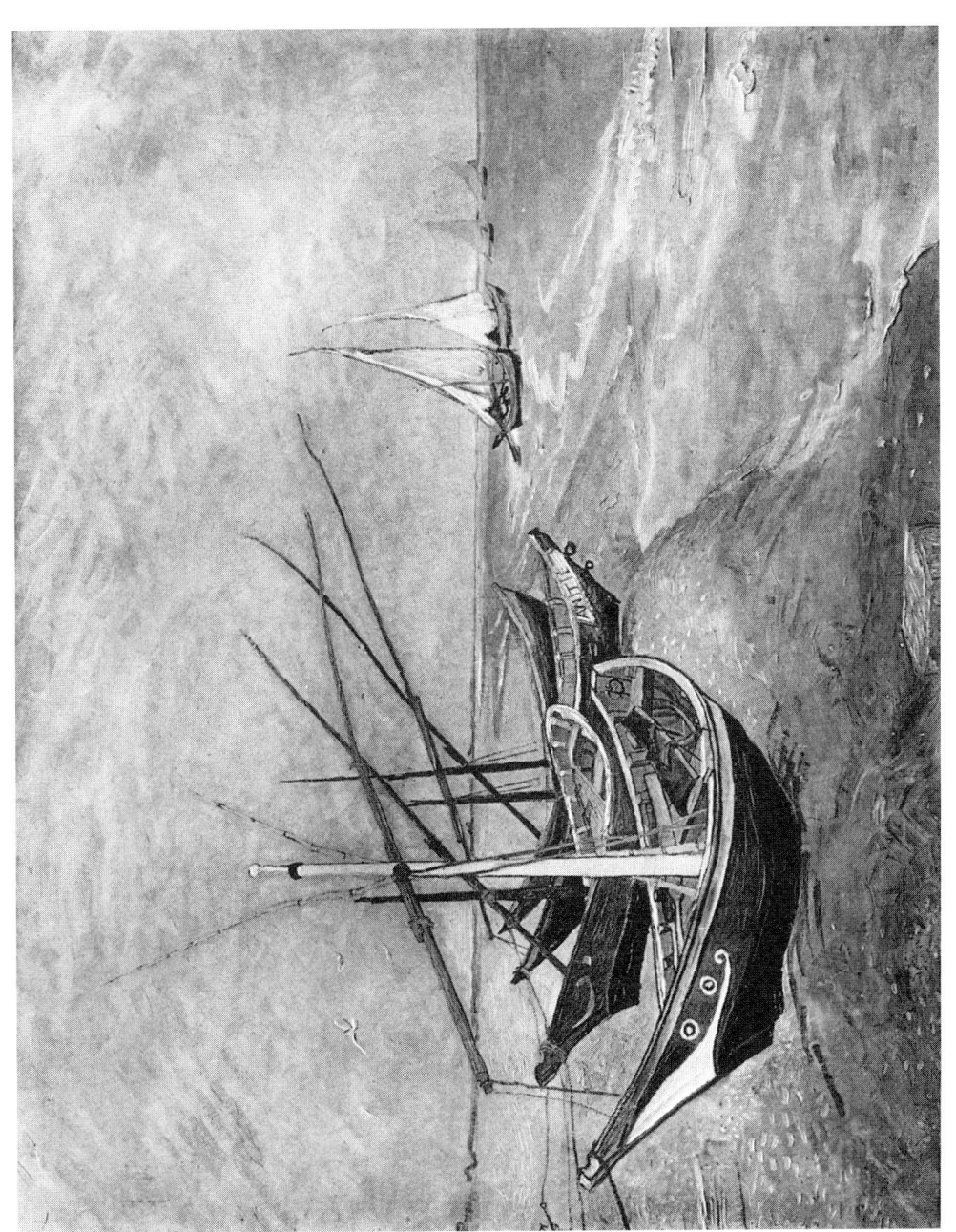

BOATS ON THE BEACH AT SAINTES MARIES

¹ From *Letters to Theo* Nos. 494–500, it is apparent that Vincent went to Saintes-Maries about 10th June. As he says he has "spent a week" there it seems clear that this letter probably dates from the third week in June. It is written on a sheet of plain white paper measuring 9 × 7 inches (23 × 18 cm.).

² *Juge de paix*, Justice of the Peace, in normal French.

³ A French daily newspaper.

⁴ He has here made two little drawings in the text to illustrate his point. *Vide* Plate 12.

⁵ Saintes-Maries de la mer, a village on the Mediterranean coast 25 miles due south of Arles. It derives its name from the "Three Marys", *i.e.* Mary, wife of Cleophas and sister of the Virgin; Mary Salome, mother of the Apostles James and John; and Mary Magdalene. According to the legend they landed there in A.D. 45 with Martha, Lazarus and Maximin and converted Provence to Christianity. A chapel over the apse of the Church contains the relics of the first two Marys, and in the crypt are the remains of their black servant Sarah. The relics of St. Sarah are an object of special devotion on the part of the gypsies and enormous gypsy pilgrimages to this shrine take place each year on 24th–25th May and 22nd October. *Vide Van Gogh and John Russell: an unpublished correspondence*, by Henry Thannhauser, Letter II, *Burlington Magazine*, September 1938: "I have been to the seaside for a week." The letter also contains a drawing identical with Plate 15.

⁶ de la Faille Nos. 413 and 414: *vide* Plates 13 and 14. This letter apparently contained two sheets of drawings and on the back of one of them was the STILL LIFE WITH THE COFFEE POT mentioned in the previous letter, *vide* p. 31.

⁷ Plates 15 and 16.

⁸ It is not certain what he is referring to, but it is probably to the sketch of houses; *vide* Plates 17 and 18.

⁹ Eugène Fromentin (1820–76), a French painter and writer. He took his subject matter from Algeria and the deserts of North Africa.

¹⁰ Jean Léon Gérôme (1824–1904), painter and sculptor; his subject-matter is, on the whole, similar to that of Fromentin.

VII

My dear Bernard,

Excuse my writing in a hurry, I'm afraid my letter won't be legible at all, but I want to answer you at once.

You know we've been very silly, Gauguin, you and I, not all going to the same place. But when Gauguin set out I wasn't sure of being able to get away, and when you set out there was that wretched question of money and you were put off by the bad news I had given you of the cost here.

It would have been more sensible if we had all set out together for Arles: for the three of us would have done the housekeeping. And now that I have had some experience of it I am beginning to see the advantages of this place. Personally I feel much better here than in the north. I even work in the wheatfields, in the full midday sun, without any protection whatever, so there you are: I bask in it like the crickets. My God, *if only I'd known this country at the age of 25 instead of 35.* At that time my passion was for greyness or rather drabness, I was always dreaming about Millet,[2] and my friends in Holland were the kind of painters like Mauve,[3] Israëls,[4] etc.

Here's a sketch of a sower[5]: big ploughed field with clods of earth, most of which is frankly violet.

A field of ripe wheat, yellow ochre in tone with a little crimson.

The sky is chrome yellow, almost as bright as the sun itself which is chrome yellow No. 1 with a little white, whereas the rest of the sky is chrome yellow Nos. 1 and 2 mixed. So it's very yellow.

The sower's blouse is blue and his trousers white.

It's a square canvas of 25.[6]

There are many echoes of the yellow in the soil, neutral tones resulting from the blending of the violet with the yellow; but I haven't taken much trouble about the truth of the colouring. I'd rather produce the sort of naïve pictures one sees in the old almanacks, in the rural calendars for example, with the hail, snow, rain or fine weather shown in a completely primitive style such as Anquetin used so successfully in his *Harvest*.

38

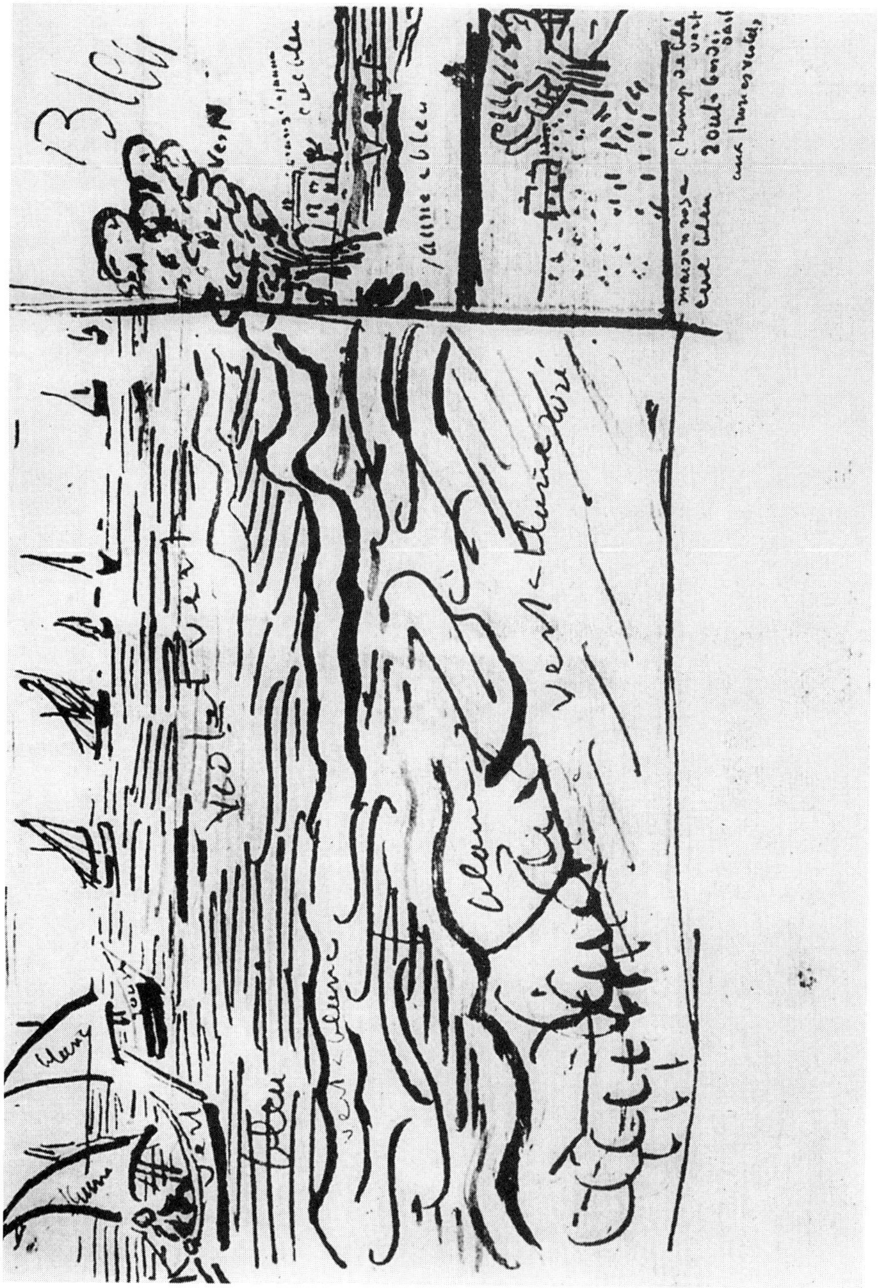

PLATE 15

FACSIMILE FROM LETTER VI

PLATE 16

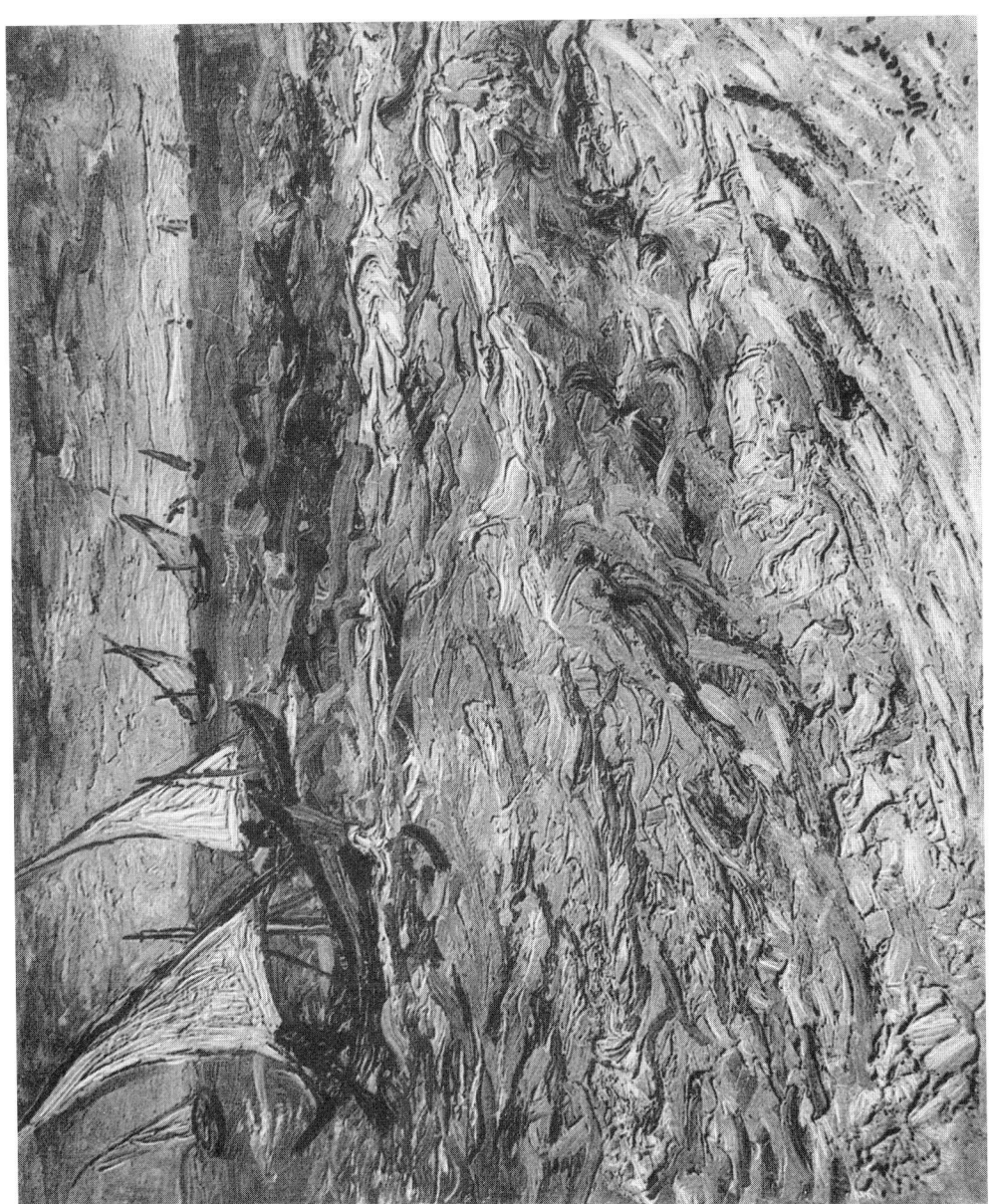

BOATS ON THE SEA AT SAINTES MARIES

I can't disguise from you the fact that I like the country, having been brought up there—floods of memories of the past, aspirations towards that infinity, of which the sower and the sheaves are symbols, enchant me now as then. But I wonder when I'll get my starry sky[7] done, a picture which haunts me always. Alas! Alas! It is just as our excellent friend Cyprien says in J. K. Huysmans' *'En Ménage'*[8]: "the best pictures are always those one dreams of when one is smoking a pipe in bed, but which never get done."

But still one ought to try, however incompetent one may feel before the unspeakable perfection and radiant splendour of nature.

How I'd love to see the sketch you have made of a brothel.

I'm continually reproaching myself for still not having done any figure studies here.

Here's another landscape[9]: Setting Sun? Rising Moon?

A summer sun anyway.

Town violet, orb yellow, sky blue-green. The wheat contains every possible shade: old gold, copper, green and red gold, yellow gold, yellow bronze, red-green.

Canvas of 30, square.

I painted it with the *mistral*[10] raging, my easel fixed to the ground with iron stakes, a trick I recommend to you. One sticks the legs of the easel firmly into the ground, then by their side one drives in an iron stake about 2 ft. long: then one binds them all together with cords. Like that you can work in a wind.[11]

What I meant about black and white[12] amounts to this. Take for example THE SOWER. The picture is divided in two: the upper part yellow, the lower part violet. Now the white trousers serve to appease and distract the eye at the moment when it would become irritated by the excessively violent contrast of yellow and violet. Now do you get my meaning?

I have got to know here a second lieutenant of the Zouaves called Milliet. I give him drawing lessons—with my perspective frame[13]—and, by Jove, I've seen many worse than the drawings he's beginning to produce. He's keen to learn, has been to Tonkin, etc. . . . He's off to Africa in October. If you were in the Zouaves he'd take you with him,

39

and would guarantee you a relatively large amount of freedom for painting in exchange for your help with his artistic problems. Does this seem to you of any use? If so, *let me know as soon as possible.*

One reason for working is that pictures are worth money. I'm sure you'll say at once that this reason is thoroughly prosaic, because you don't believe it. At the same time it's true that one reason for not working is that the actual canvas and paints merely cost us money, while we're waiting.

But still drawings don't cost much.

Gauguin too is bored at Pont-Aven and complains like you of his isolation. Why not go and see him? But then I'm not sure he's going to stay there: and I think he intends going back to Paris. He says he thought you would have gone to Pont-Aven. My God, if only we were all three here together. I know you think it's too far. But then *what about the winter*: here one can work all the year round. I like this countryside because I have less to fear from the cold which, by stopping my blood circulating, stops me thinking or doing anything.

You'll be able to judge for yourself when you're a soldier.

You'll lose your melancholy, which may very well come from your having too little blood, or being in poor condition, which, however, I don't really believe.

It's the blasted foul wine of Paris and the filthy fat of the beef-steaks which do it. I had reached a state where my blood had given up functioning, it literally wasn't functioning at all. Anyway after only four weeks here it began to work again: but during just that time, my friend, I had a fit of depression like yours, from which I should surely have suffered as much, had I not welcomed it with pleasure, as a sure sign that I would get better—which in fact actually happened.

So stay in the country instead of going back to Paris, for you'll need all your strength to come through the trials of your trip to Africa properly. And the more blood, good blood, you have beforehand, the better for you, because it's probably difficult to get in condition down there in the heat.

Painting and making love aren't compatible, it saps the brain, that's what's such a bore.

PLATE 17

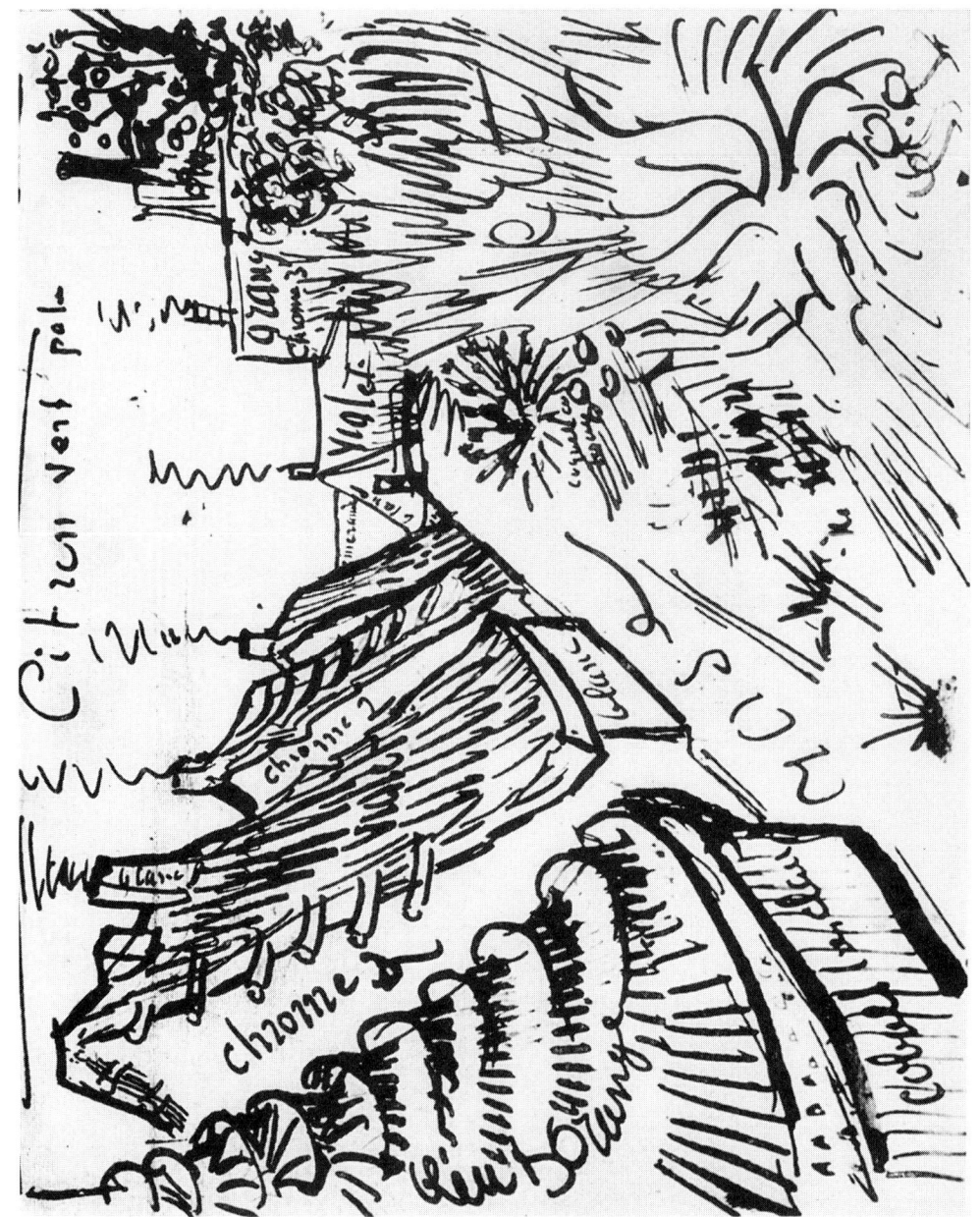

FACSIMILE FROM LETTER VI

PLATE 18

HOUSES AT SAINTES MARIES

As you know the symbol of St. Luke, the patron saint of painters, is an *ox*. So one must be as patient as an ox if one wants to work in the field of art. But the bulls are very happy not having to work at filthy painting.

What I have been trying to say is this: after your fit of depression you'll be stronger than before, your health will improve and you'll find nature so beautiful around you that your only desire will be to paint.

I think too that your poetry will change like your painting. After an eccentric beginning you have now started to write things which have a sort of *Egyptian* calm and great simplicity.

> *Que l'heure est donc brève*
> *Qu'on passe en aimant*
> *C'est moins qu'un instant*
> *Un peu plus qu'un rêve.*
> *Le temps nous enlève*
> *Notre enchantement.*[14]

That's not by Baudelaire, I don't even know who wrote it: they're the words of a song in Daudet's '*Nabab*'[15]—at least that's where I've taken it from—but doesn't it say something *as effectively as a real lady with a mere shrug of the shoulders.*

I've been reading recently Loti's '*Madame Chrysanthème*'[16]: it gives an interesting picture of Japan. Just now my brother is having an exhibition of Claude Monet[17]: I'd like to see it. Among others Guy de Maupassant[18] came to have a look and from now on he says he'll be a frequent visitor to the Boulevard Montmartre.[19]

I must go and paint, so I must finish. I'll probably write again in a day or two. Please excuse my not having put enough stamps on my letter, but I took it myself *to the post office, and it's not the first time that it's happened to me here, even after enquiring at the post-office when I was doubtful, that my letter was insufficiently stamped.* You've no idea of the carelessness and nonchalance of the local people. But anyway, you'll soon be experiencing all that yourself in Africa. Thanks for your letter. I hope to write again soon, when I'm in less of a hurry.

A handshake,

Yours,

Vincent.

[1] This letter seems to have been written directly after Vincent's return from Saintes-Maries, *i.e.* about 20th June. *Letters to Theo* No. 498, before the visit to Saintes-Maries, first mentions the Monet Exhibition: in Letter 501 he says that Bernard has written complaining of feeling lonesome. The latter half of the present letter is the answer. This letter is written on a plain sheet of white paper measuring $10\frac{1}{2} \times 8\frac{1}{4}$ inches (27 by 21 cm.).

[2] Jean François Millet (1815–75), French landscape painter, one of the leaders of the Barbizon School and a great friend of Théodore Rousseau. Painted scenes of peasant life, one of the most famous of which is *The Angelus.*

[3] Anton Mauve (1838–88), a Dutch painter, in style like Millet, cousin of van Gogh through his mother, and one of van Gogh's teachers at The Hague when he lived there in 1882. It was in Mauve's studio that van Gogh threw the plaster casts into the coal-bin screaming: "Man, do not speak to me again about plaster, for I cannot stand it." Despite this incident, however, Vincent never lost his admiration for Mauve as an artist and when the latter died he painted for his widow the picture *Souvenir de Mauve,* de la Faille No. 394; *vide Letters to Theo,* Nos. 472 and 474.

[4] Josef Israëls (1824–1911), a Dutch counterpart to Millet and leader of the younger painters in The Hague.

[5] *Vide* Plates 19 and 20: the finished picture is de la Faille No. 422; *vide Letters to Theo* No. 501. He writes to Russell also "I am working at a Sower" and sends him a drawing similar to the present one; *vide Van Gogh and John Russell: an unpublished correspondence,* Letter II: by Henry Thannhauser in the *Burlington Magazine,* September 1938.

42

PLATE 19

FACSIMILE FROM LETTER VII

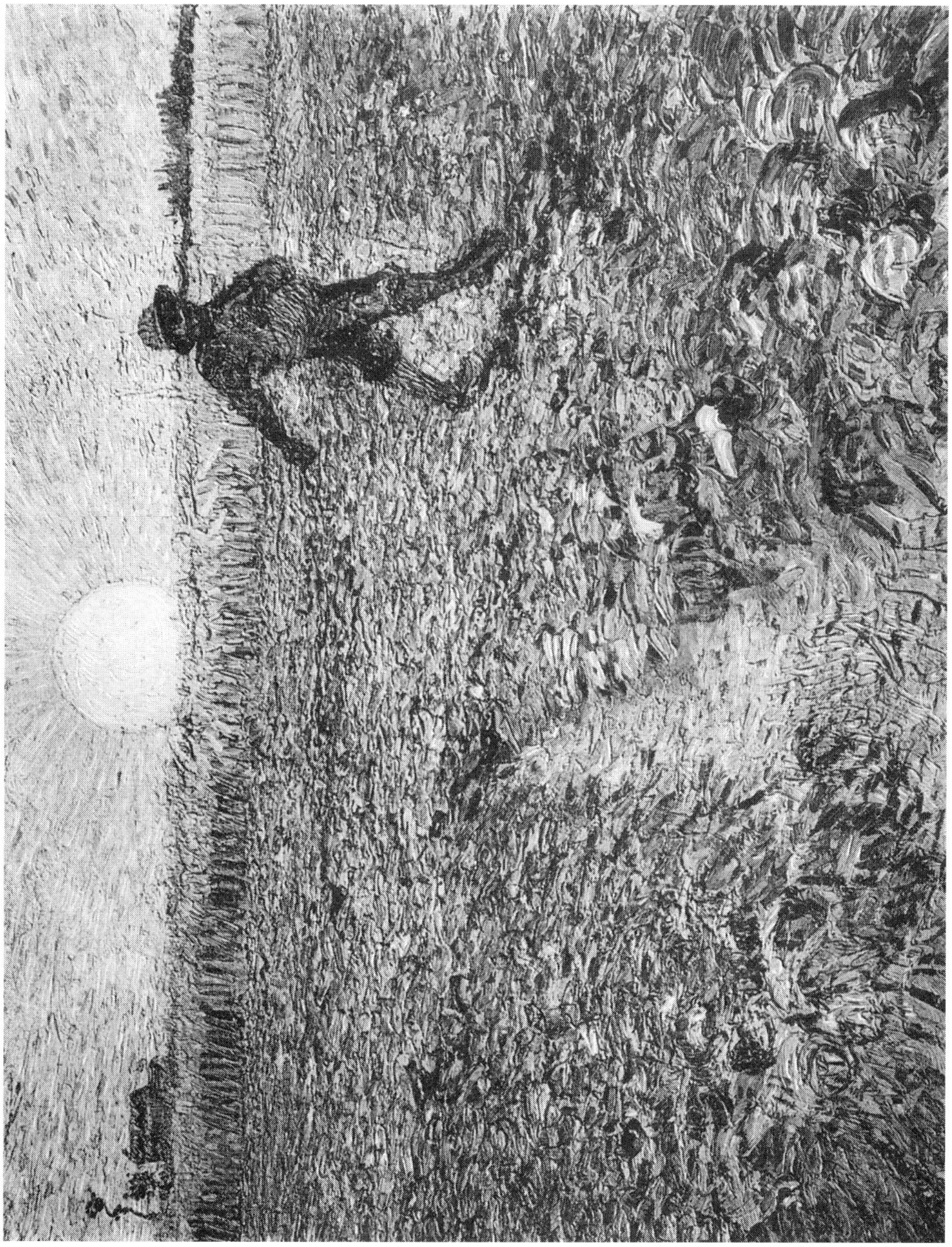

PLATE 20

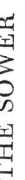

THE SOWER

[6] French canvases are known by their sizes. The following table shows the measurements in each category:

Size	Landscape cm	Figure cm	Seascape cm	Size	Landscape cm	Figure cm	Seascape cm
4	33×24	33×22	33×19	12	61×50	61×46	61×38
5	35×27	35×24	35×22	15	65×54	65×50	65×46
6	41×33	41×27	41×24	20	73×60	73×54	73×50
8	46×38	46×33	46×27	25	81×65	81×60	81×54
10	55×46	55×38	55×33	30	92×73	92×65	92×60

[7] *Vide* LETTER III.

[8] Joris Karl Huysmans (1848–1907), French novelist, descended from a family of artists of Dutch extraction. He was for thirty years in the Ministry of the Interior. '*En Ménage*', a novel of everyday life, was written in 1881. He also wrote a study of the Impressionist movement, '*L'Art Moderne*' (1883).

[9] Plates 21 and 22: the finished picture is de la Faille No. 468; *vide* also LETTER IX, and *Letters to Theo* No. 535.

[10] Very strong, dry, cold wind from the north which is prevalent in the south-east part of France.

[11] *Vide* Plate 21, where he illustrates this with a drawing.

[12] *Vide* LETTER VI.

[13] van Gogh refers to "*mon cadre perspectif*": he should more accurately have written, "*mon cadre de mise au carré*". It was a contraption made by van Gogh himself and of which, according to Emile Bernard, he made great use in the early days. It was simply a canvas chassis (without canvas) across which had been stretched strings at regular intervals, running vertically and horizontally. This formed several little squares, and Vincent apparently studied his subject through this and thus was able to reproduce it accurately on his canvas. Later on, of course, when he allowed his emotions more freedom, he abandoned it.

[14] "How short is the hour one passes in loving, it is less than an instant but a little more than a dream. Time takes our enchantment away from us."

[15] '*Le Nabab*', a novel by Daudet, written in 1877.

[16] Julien Viaud (called Pierre) Loti (1850–1923), a French naval officer and later, novelist, author of '*Madame Chrysanthème*': his subjects are usually exotic and his work profoundly melancholy.

[17] *Vide Letters to Theo* Nos. 498 and 501.

[18] Guy de Maupassant (1850–93), French novelist of the realist school.

[19] Theo van Gogh was manager of the firm of Boussod and Valadon, successor to the firm of Goupil, whose gallery was in the Boulevard Montmartre.

My dear Bernard,

It's fine that you're reading the Bible. I start off with this because I've always restrained myself from recommending it to you. I have often stopped involuntarily when reading one of the many sayings of Moses, Saint Luke, etc., and thought to myself that's all he needs: there you are now in the middle of it . . . the artistic neurosis.

For the study of Christ produces it inevitably, and especially in me, where it is complicated by so many blocked pipes.

The Bible is Christ, for the Old Testament leads up to this peak. St. Paul and the Evangelists lie on the other slope of the sacred mountain.

What a little story it is! Well, there we are! It's only the Jews in this world who begin by declaring anything which is not of them defiled.

The other peoples under the great sun of those parts, the Egyptians, the Indians, the Ethiopians: Babylon, Nineveh, what a pity they haven't got such carefully written records! Anyway the study of them is fine, and being able to read anything would be tantamount to not being able to read at all.

But the consolation in this Bible, which distresses us and yet relieves our despair and our indignation—it really does hurt us and outrages us by its pettiness and contagious madness[2]—the consolation it contains, like a kernel inside a hard shell, a bitter pulp, is Christ.

Christ, as I feel him, has only really been expressed in paint by Delacroix and Rembrandt . . . after that there's Millet, who painted Christ's teaching.

All other religious painting makes me smile rather—at the religion, not at the painting. Take the Italian primitives, say Botticelli, or the Flemish primitives, say van Eyck, or the Germans such as Cranach: why, they are all pagans and they only interest me on the same plane as the Greeks, Velazquez and many other such naturalistic artists.

Christ alone of all the philosophers, magicians, etc., took as his principal theme the certainty of eternal life, the endlessness of time,

PLATE 21

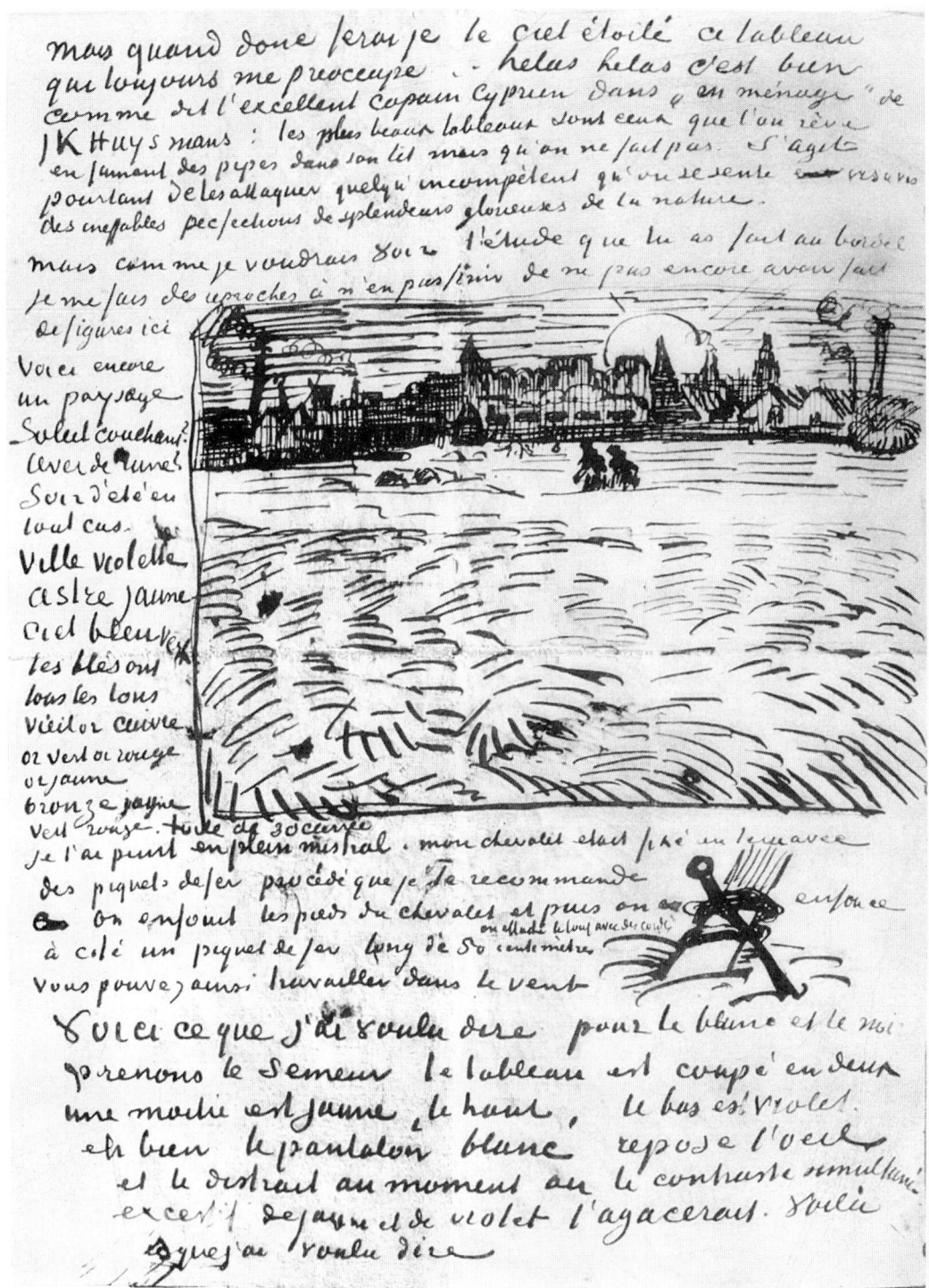

FACSIMILE FROM LETTER VII

PLATE 22

VIEW OF ARLES AT SUNSET

the nothingness of death, the need for and the justification of calmness and devotion. He lived a serene life, *and was the greatest artist of all, disdaining marble, clay or colour, working with living flesh.*

That is to say that this unbelievable artist, one who is scarcely conceivable to such an obtuse instrument as the modern neurotic, worn-out brain, made neither statues, nor pictures, nor books; indeed, he said clearly enough what he was doing—*fashioning living men,* immortal beings.

And that's serious, the more so because it's true.

He didn't write books either: indeed he would be disgusted with the literature of Christianity as a whole, for there are very few literary productions that can stand beside the Gospel of St. Luke or the Epistles of St. Paul—so simple in their hard, warlike form. Christ, this great artist, though he disdained books written about ideas (sensations) never, on the other hand, disdained the spoken word—*especially in the form of parables.* (The sower, the harvest, the fig-tree, etc.)

And who would dare to say he lied the day when, scornfully fore-telling the collapse of Rome, he declared: Heaven and earth shall pass away, but my words shall not pass away.[3]

These spoken words, which, like a great prodigal lord, he did not deign even to write down, are one of the highest peaks, the highest in fact ever reached by art, which there becomes a creative force, a pure creative force.

Such considerations as these, my dear Bernard, take us a long way, a very long way: *they raise us even above art.* They enable one to catch a glimpse of the art of creating life, the art of living immortality.

And they're not irrelevant to painting.

The patron saint of painters, St. Luke himself, doctor, painter and Evangelist, whose symbol alas is nothing better than an ox, is there to encourage us. Yet in our real, true life we painters are quite humble, vegetating under the crushing yoke of a profession which is scarcely practicable on this thankless planet, on whose surface "the love of art means loss of true love."[4]

But as there's no proof to the contrary—and presupposing, of course, in the innumerable other planets and suns, the existence of lines, forms and colours—we are free to maintain a certain cheerfulness with regard to the possibility of painting under better and changed conditions of existence, an existence changed by a phenomenon no more tricky or astonishing than the transformation of a caterpillar into a butterfly, or of a white grub into a cockchafer.

The field of action of our metamorphosed butterfly-painter would be one of the many stars which, after death, are probably no more inaccessible to us than the little black dots on maps which, in our terrestrial existence, stand for towns and villages.[5]

Science, scientific reasoning rather, seems to me an instrument with a great future.

For look: the earth was thought to be *flat*. Indeed, it was true: between Paris and Asnières,[6] for example, it still is today.

But that hasn't prevented scientists proving conclusively that the world is round. And no one contests it.

In spite of this there's still an idea that life runs *in a flat progression* from birth to death.

But life too is probably *round*, and far greater in extent and capacity than the hemisphere which we know at present.

Future generations will probably enlighten us on this interesting subject: then will be the turn of Science, if she likes, to draw conclusions more or less parallel to the sayings of Christ, dealing with the other half of our existence.

However, all we really know is that we are painters living a real life and that we must go on drawing breath as long as we have breath to draw.

How lovely is Eug[ène] Delacroix's *Christ in the boat on the Sea[7] of Gennesaret.*[8] Jesus asleep, surrounded by a pale lemon coloured halo, shines out against the dramatic violet, dark blue and blood-red of the group of speechless disciples, while the terrible emerald coloured sea rises up and out of the frame. It's a work of genius, I'd make you some sketches of it if I weren't so worn out, having been drawing and painting with a model—a Zouave—for three or four days: writing on the other hand rests and distracts me.

What I have turned out is very ugly: a drawing of the Zouave

PLATE 23

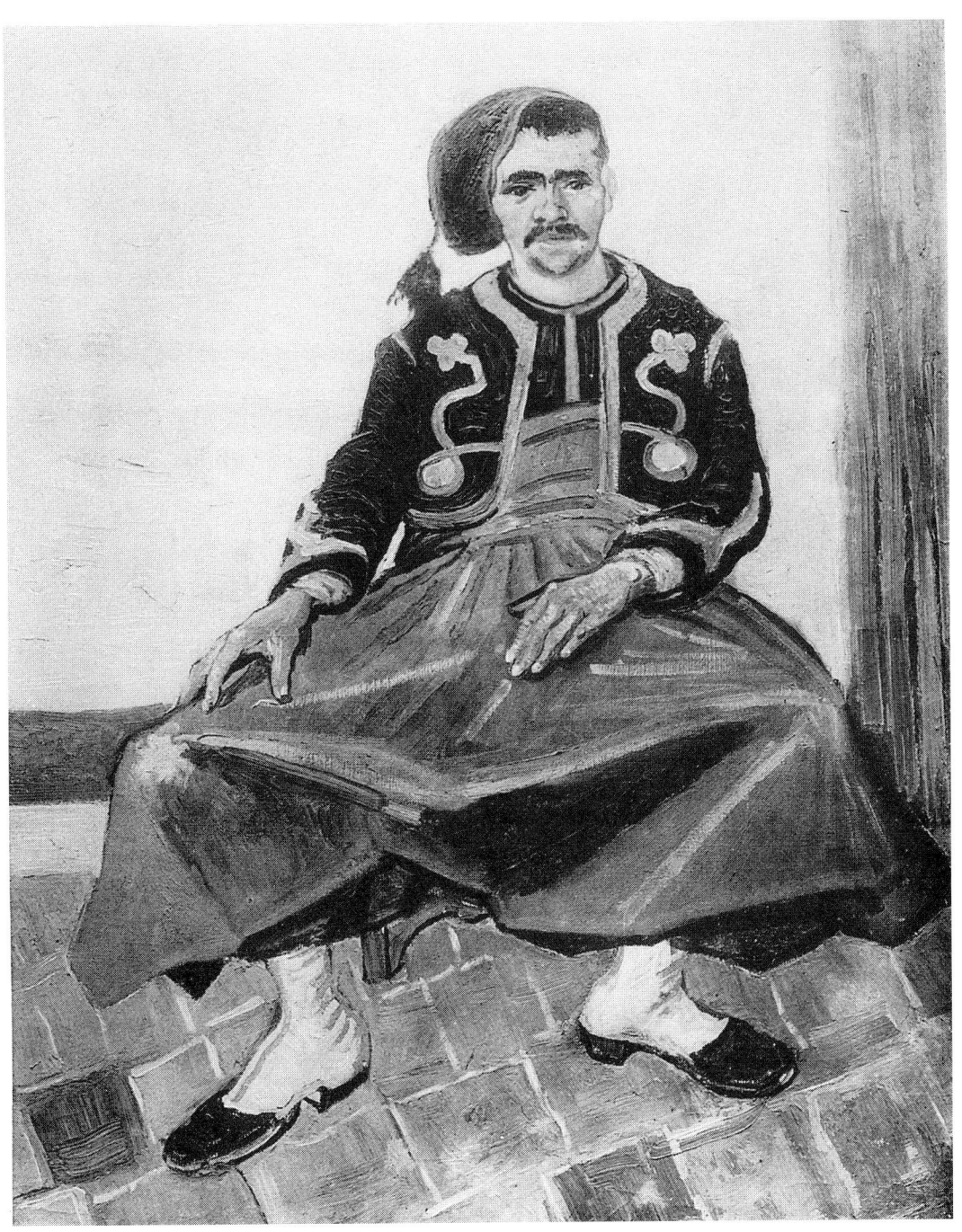

THE ZOUAVE

seated, an oil sketch of the Zouave against a perfectly white wall,[9] and lastly a portrait of him against a green door with some orange bricks of a wall. They are all hard, and anyhow *ugly* and unsuccessful. All the same, as real difficulties have been tackled, they may open up the path for the future.

The figures I do almost always seem to me horrid, not to mention how they seem to others; and yet it is the study of figures which is the most stimulating if one sets about it in a different way from that taught by M. Benjamin Constant,[10] for example.

I was very pleased to get your letter, and *your sketch was very very interesting:* thank you very much. One of these days I will send you a drawing myself: tonight I'm too worn out, my eyes are tired, even if my brain isn't.

Do you happen to remember Puvis'[11] *St. John Baptist?* I find it stunning and as *marvellous* as Eug[ène] Delacroix.

The passage you dug up in the Gospels about St. John the Baptist expresses just what you yourself have seen in him. Lots of people scrambling round a figure asking "Are you the Christ? Are you Elias?": just as nowadays they might press round the Impressionists, or one of the more experimental members, saying "Have you found the way?" It's just like that.

Just now my brother has an exhibition of Claude Monet[12]—10 pictures painted between February and May at Antibes[13]: it's lovely it seems.

Have you ever read a life of Luther? Cranach, Dürer and Holbein are part of *him. He—his personality*—is the high light of the Middle Ages.

I don't like the Roi-Soleil[14] any more than you do—in fact to me he's more like a fire-extinguisher, your Louis XIV—he's altogether a bore, this kind of Methodist Solomon.[15] I don't like Solomon either, and the Methodists too not at all. Solomon seems to me to have been a hypocritical pagan, I have no respect at all for his kind of architecture, an imitation of other styles, and still less for his writing: the pagans did better than that.

What's the latest situation as to your military service? Do you or don't you want me to speak to the 2nd Lieutenant in the Zouaves? Are you going to Africa or not? And is it counted double time if you do it in Africa? But, look to the state of your blood: with anæmia one doesn't progress, least of all with one's painting: you should try and cultivate a really tough character, the sort which assures one a long life, then try a thoroughly monastic life, only visiting the brothel once a fortnight—that's what I do, it's not exactly poetic, but I realise that it is my duty to subordinate my private life to my painting.

If we happen to be in the Louvre together, I should like to look at the primitives with you.

Personally, when I am in the Louvre, I still go regularly to look at the Dutch school, and especially Rembrandt. Rembrandt I once studied very carefully—then there's Potter[16] for example, who, on a small panel of 4 or 6[17] paints a single white stallion, neighing and bucking in a meadow all alone under a heavy stormy sky, lost in the rich green immensity of the fragrant meadows. There are marvels in these old Dutch masters which can be compared to nothing else.

A handshake; and once more thanks for your letter and the sketch.

Yours,

Vincent.

PS. The sonnets seem to be going well: that is to say, the colour is good, the line less strong, or rather less assured, the design hesitant—I can't find the right word—the moral aim not at all clear.

[1] The references later in the letter to the two portraits of the Zouave relate this letter to *Letters to Theo* Nos. 501 and 502, which were written at the end of June. But in addition, the further reference to the Monet Exhibition suggests that it was written not long after LETTER VII, while the mention of his having received a letter with a sketch connects it definitely with Letter 502. This letter is written on a plain sheet of white paper measuring 10 × 8 inches (27 × 20.5 cm.).

[2] *"folie contagieuse."*

[3] St. Matthew XXIV, v. 35.

[4] *"L'amour de l'art fait perdre l'amour vrai"*: a quotation from Richepin, a contemporary poet; cf. *Letters to Theo* No. 462.

[5] This image occurs also at the end of *Letters to Theo* No. 506, written about 1st July.

[6] A suburb on the north side of Paris: Vincent used to go and paint there with Bernard during 1887, at the studio given to Bernard by his parents.

[7] There are many versions of this: *vide* Robaut *L'Oeuvre Complète d'Eugène Delacroix*, Nos. 1214–1220.

[8] Vincent uses the word *mer*.

[9] Plate 23. There has been a good deal of confusion over the question of whether Vincent painted more Zouaves than one. The paintings referred to here, de la Faille Nos. 423 and 424, and the drawing No. 1443, are all of the same person, but this is not the same as the person depicted in officer's uniform on de la Faille No. 473, who is Milliet. *Vide Letters to Theo* Nos. 501 and 502, where the Zouave is described as having "the neck of a bull and the eye of a tiger". The same model also appears on de la Faille (drawings) No. 1482, which is mentioned later and which is dedicated: *"A mon cher copain Emile Bernard"*.

[10] Benjamin Constant (1845–1902), a historical painter and portraitist.

[11] Puvis de Chavannes.

[12] *Vide Letters to Theo* No. 498; cf. LETTER VII Note 17.

[13] A town on the Mediterranean coast not far from Cannes.

[14] Louis XIV, King of France.

[15] Emile Bernard disclaims holding such views.

[16] Paulus Potter (1625–54), a Dutch landscape and animal painter.

[17] *Vide* LETTER VII Note 6.

My dear Bernard,

I have no idea what I stuffed into my letter yesterday instead of the sheet herewith, which deals with your last sonnet. The trouble is I'm so worn out with work that in the evening, although writing is a relief to me, I am like a machine out of gear, for a day spent in the full sun has so taxed another side of me. That's why I stuffed in some other sheet instead of the present one.

Reading over again yesterday's effort, I'm just sending it along as it stands, it seems to me legible and so I'm sending it to you.

Today another day of real hard work. I wonder what you would say to my new canvases. You won't find a trace of the timid, conscientious brush-stroke of Cézanne. But as, at the moment, I'm painting the same landscape, the Crau² and Camargue,³ although a slightly different part of it, there may well be a certain similarity in colour. I don't know. Involuntarily I have thought of Cézanne from time to time, particularly at moments when I have realised how clumsy—permit me the word clumsy—is his touch in certain studies: of course he probably did them with the *mistral* raging. But as half the time I am faced with the same difficulty I can understand why Cézanne's touch is sometimes so very sure, and sometimes seems so clumsy. It's because his easel rocks.

Sometimes I work terribly fast. Is it a fault? I can't help it.

The large canvas of 30, for example, *The Summer Evening*⁴ was painted at one sitting.

I can't work on it again: shall I destroy it? Why should I? I went out specially to do it while the *mistral* was raging.

It's more the intensity of thought than the tranquillity of touch we are after: but in circumstances such as these where one is driven to work impulsively, on the spot and directly from nature, I doubt whether it is always possible to preserve a calm well-ordered touch. After all it's rather like being suddenly assaulted with a rapier.

I have sent your drawing to my brother and begged him to buy something from you.⁵

If he *can* I'm sure my brother will buy, for he knows well how keen I am that you should sell something.

If you like I would set aside to exchange with you the head of the Zouave which I have painted.

Only we won't discuss it unless at the same time I can sell something for you.

It would be in return for your sketch of the brothel. I'm sure if we were to do a picture of a brothel *together* that we would use my sketch of the Zouave for one of the figures. What a pity there aren't several painters inclined to collaborate and do great things.

Perhaps we will see that happen with the artists of the future. There would have to be several of us to cope with the material difficulties of the paintings which are *essential* to today.

Anyhow we haven't got there yet, alas: painting doesn't move as fast as literature.

I'm writing to you now, like yesterday, in great haste, quite worn out: in fact at the moment I'm not even capable of drawing, I'm so utterly weary after my morning's work in the fields.

The sun down here is very tiring indeed. And I'm quite incapable of judging my own work. I can't see whether the sketches are good or bad. I have seven studies of wheatfields; all of them unfortunately, and very much against my will, merely landscapes. Yellow landscapes, old gold, done quickly, quickly, quickly, and urgently like the harvester, who works silently in the blazing sun, concentrating on his work.

I daresay you are a bit surprised perhaps to see how little I like the Bible, though I have often tried to study it. It is only the kernel Christ, who, artistically speaking, seems to me to rise above, or at any rate *to differ from* the figures of Greek, Indian, Egyptian or Persian antiquity: and they went a long way. But Christ, I repeat, is more of an artist than anyone, he works in the spirit and the living flesh, he creates men not statues. Well . . . I feel really like an ox—being myself a painter— and I respect the Bull,[6] the Eagle and the Man to an extent which will prevent my becoming ambitious. A handshake,

Yours,

Vincent.

51

PS.[7] Let me add an explanation of what I mean by saying of your sonnets: "the line has not much self-assurance".

At the end you point a moral.

You say to Society that it is rotten because the prostitute is like so much meat in the market-place.

That's all right, the prostitute is like a piece of meat in a butcher's shop. And I, animal that I am, understand and feel that, I recognise one of my own sensations; I say to myself: that's well spoken. For the sonorous rhythm of your colourful words conjures up for me with great intensity an image of the brutal reality of the doss-house: but the reproofs to "Society" at the end make no impression on an animal like me, an expression as empty as "the Good Lord".

That's not successful, I say to myself, then sink back into the animal state and forget the poetry which at first was powerful enough to dispel my sloth.

Is that or isn't it true?

Stating facts, as you are beginning to do, is like the surgeon getting out his knife and laying bare the anatomy.

I listen and, with reflection and interest, I watch: but when, later, the anatomy professor starts pointing morals like that, then it doesn't seem to me that his final tirade is as valuable as his demonstration.

Study, analyse the social structure: that's always far more effective than moralising.

Nothing would seem more odd to me than to say, for example: Here is a piece of meat from the market; but look how, in spite of everything, it still reacts for a moment to the stimulus of a more refined, more unexpected love. Just as the sated caterpillar, when it can eat no more, deserts the cabbage leaf to crawl along the wall, so this woman, who has had her fill, is unable to love any more, even if she tries. She is seeking, seeking all the while: but does she herself know what? She is conscious, living, sensitive, galvanised, momentarily revived, but powerless.

However, she can still love, therefore she is alive, there's no denying it, although she is finished and nearing the end of her bestial existence on this earth. Where was this butterfly hatched?—this butterfly lately a sated caterpillar, this cockchafer lately a white grub?

Well, that's where I've got to in my study of old tarts. I wish I too knew as accurately whose larva I am.

[1] This was written the day after LETTER VIII: cf. *Letters to Theo* Nos. 502 and 503. This letter is written on a large sheet, 10 × 8 inches (27 × 20.5 cm.) and a small sheet of plain white paper 8 × 5 inches (20.5 × 13.2 cm.).

[2] The Crau: the Campus Lapideus or Cravus of the Romans; a flat stony plain, 77 square miles in area, running east and west between Arles and Aix south of the Alpilles, and composed of stones brought down from the Alpine glaciers by the river Durance. Artificial irrigation has now done something to break down the sterility of the region.

[3] The Camargue: a peninsula comprising almost the whole of the Rhône delta; it is constantly increasing with alluvial deposits. In the middle is a large lagoon, the Etang de Vaccarès; most of the peninsula consists of reedy swamps, barren saltings and dunes on which grow junipers, stone-pines and tamarinds. On the pasture-land further away from the sea, mounted herdsmen guard half-wild herds of small, black cattle (sometimes used for bull-fighting) and small pale, grey horses. Saintes-Maries is at the extremity of the Camargue.

[4] *Vide* LETTER VII, Note 9.

[5] *Vide Letters to Theo* Nos. 502 and 503. It would appear that this was a drawing of a brothel: on the back of it was "a poem . . . in just the same tone as the drawing". Vincent addressed it in error to his brother's first address in Paris: 54 Rue de Laval; the letter was returned to him, having been opened, at Arles and he sent it again to Theo at the correct address.

[6] Curiously enough van Gogh uses here the words *"taureau"* and *"homme"*: he is referring, of course, to the symbols of the Evangelists—St. Luke and the Ox, St. Matthew and the Angel (not the "Man" as he incorrectly writes), St. Mark and the Lion (not, of course, the "Bull"), St. John and the Eagle.

[7] This is written on the smaller sheet of paper and is the enclosure mentioned earlier: it concerns the poem on the back of the drawing.

X

Dear old Bernard,

You will perhaps be inclined to forgive me for not having replied to your letter immediately when you see that I am sending you a few sketches with this one.

The one of *The Garden* has something of the spirit of:—

Des tapis velus

De fleurs et de verdures tissus,[2]

by Crevelli[3] or Virelli, it doesn't matter much which.

Well, anyway, I was determined my pen should reply to your quotations, but not with mere words. Today, moreover, I haven't got much of a head for discussion as I am up to my eyes in work.

I've done some large ink drawings. Actually two: an enormous stretch of flat country, a bird's eye view seen from the top of a hill, with vines and fields of newly-cut wheat.[4] All that carried on endlessly, the ground stretching away like the surface of a sea towards the horizon, where it is bounded by the little hills of the Crau.

It doesn't look Japanese, yet actually it is the most Japanese thing I have done: a microscopic figure of a labourer, a little train cutting across the wheatfields—those are all the signs of life there are in it.

Now listen: a few days after I started going there I was talking to a painter friend of mine who said "That would be a bore to do."[5] I didn't say anything: I found it so astounding I hadn't even the strength to swear at the idiot. I go back and back, again and again. It's fine! I have two drawings of it—this flat landscape where there is nothing but . . . infinity . . . eternity.

Well, while I was drawing a fellow came up, not a painter but a soldier. "Does it surprise you," I said, "that I find that as beautiful as the sea?"

But he knew the sea, that fellow. "No," he said, "I'm not surprised that you find it as beautiful as the sea: but myself I find it *even more* beautiful than the sea, because it's *inhabited.*"

Which of the observers was more the artist, the first or the second,

54

the painter or the soldier? Personally I prefer the soldier's eye, don't you?

Now it's my turn to say to you: answer quickly—this time by return of post. I want to know if you will agree to making me some sketches of your Breton studies. I have a packet which is about to be sent off, but before it goes I want to do for you at least half a dozen new ink sketches of *motifs*.

Having little doubt but that you will do anything for your friends, I for my part am beginning work without even waiting for your answer. You see, I want to send these sketches to my brother to persuade him to take some of them for our collection.

As a matter of fact I have already written to him about them: but we have something on our hands at the moment which has left us absolutely without a farthing.

The truth is that Gauguin, who has been very ill,[6] is probably coming to spend next winter with me in the south. And it's a question of paying his journey. Once here, my God, well two can live cheaper than one. That's another reason why I want some of your things here. Once Gauguin is here the two of us will try and arrange something in Marseilles, we'll probably have an exhibition there. Now I'd like to have some of your things here too, though I don't want to spoil your chances of a sale in Paris. Anyway, I don't think I can be depriving you of anything by persuading you to make a mutual exchange of painted studies. And as soon as I can I'll buy something more, but things are difficult at the moment.

One thing is sure, that if, sooner or later, Gauguin and I have an exhibition you will have to send some things too. Thomas[7] has finally bought Anquetin's study *The Peasant*.

A cordial handshake; till soon again and

Yours,

Vincent.

¹ The connections between the present letter and *Letters to Theo* Nos. 509–511 would seem to establish this date. This letter is written on a sheet of white paper measuring $8\frac{1}{4} \times 5\frac{1}{2}$ inches (21 × 13.5 cm.), ruled in a network of squares.

² "Fluffy carpets woven of flowers and greenery." These lines are quoted from the famous *Ballade* by Charles d'Orleans, beginning:

Le temps a laissé son manteau
De vent, de froidure et de pluye . . .

³ An orthographical error—he means Crivelli.

⁴ In *Letters to Theo* No. 509 (written towards the middle of July) he writes: "I think that these two I've spoken of, the flat countryside covered with vines and stubble-fields will give you an idea of it. . . . Believe me I am worn out by these drawings." Probably de la Faille, Drawings Nos. 1420 and 1424. He is discussing the Crau and Montmajour.

⁵ This story is also told in *Letters to Theo* No. 509.

⁶ He was still suffering from dysentery, caught during his trip to Panama and Martinique.

⁷ A Parisian art-dealer with a gallery on the Boulevard Malesherbe. There were a great many plans as to how he could be involved in supporting van Gogh and the Impressionists: the *Letters to Theo* are full of details. Thomas, however, soon went bankrupt and ended selling the pictures he owned from a studio in the Avenue Trudenne.

Dear old Bernard,

I have just sent you, today, 9 more sketches of things I have painted. They are the sort of *motifs* which inspire old Cézanne: for the Crau near Aix² is more or less the same landscape as that round Tarascon or the Crau here. The Camargue is more straightforward, for frequently there is nothing but poor soil with here and there a tamarind bush or some coarse grasses, which flourish in such barren surroundings like alfa-grass in the desert.

Knowing how much you like Cézanne I thought these sketches of Provence would please you; not that there's much resemblance between a drawing by Cézanne and one of mine. No more in fact than there is between me and Monticelli! But I too have a great affection for this countryside which they love so, and for the same reasons: its colour and logical design.

By the word *collaboration*³ my dear Bernard, I didn't mean that either two or several painters ought to work on the same pictures. I meant rather a variety of works which belong together and complement each other. Think of the Italian primitives, the German primitives, the Dutch school, the later Italian school: why it's the case throughout the whole history of painting.

Involuntarily works fall into "groups" or "series".

Today, for example, even the Impressionists have become a group, despite all their disastrous internal squabbles, each member getting at the other's throat with a passion worthy of a nobler and better aim.

In our northern school there's Rembrandt, who was the leader because his influence can be felt in all who came in contact with him. Take Paulus Potter, for example, who painted animals at rut or excited in equally passionate landscapes, either with a storm in progress, in sunlight, or with an autumn melancholy: yet before he met Rembrandt his work was dry and meticulous.

Here are two people who belong together like brothers: Potter and Rembrandt; yet although Rembrandt probably never added a single brush stroke to any of Potter's paintings it doesn't prevent both Potter and Ruysdael being indebted to him for their best quality, that something which is so infinitely touching when we have learnt to look at some corner of old Holland through their temperament.

Then comes the point that the material difficulties of a painter's life today make collaboration, a union of artists, desirable (as much so as in the days of the Guilds of St. Luke).[4] Material difficulties being solved, the painters existing among a band of brothers, not of backbiters, would be happier and undoubtedly less open to ridicule, less idiotic and less culpable.

Anyway, I won't insist. Life carries us off so soon, we haven't time to discuss and act as well. That's the reason why, with the union existing only in a very incomplete form today, we are each drifting on the high seas in our own wretched little skiff and facing alone the mountainous billows of our times.

Is it a case of renaissance or of decadence? We cannot judge: we are too close to things not to be misled by false perspectives. Our eye sees contemporary happenings with their proportions exaggerated, probably in direct ratio to our misfortunes or our deserts.

A hearty handshake: I hope soon to have some news from you.

Yours,

Vincent.

---

[1] This letter must have been written quite soon after LETTER X. In *Letters to Theo* No. 511 van Gogh writes: "Today I sent six drawings from painted studies to Bernard. I have promised him six more, and I have asked for some sketches from his painted studies in exchange." The batch here referred to seems to be the second batch—"more sketches"—but he sent "nine" not "six". This letter is written on a plain sheet of white paper measuring $6\frac{3}{4} \times 4\frac{1}{4}$ inches (17.5 × 11 cm.).

[2] The Crau d'Aix is a continuation of the Crau d'Arles: *vide* LETTER IX Note 2.

[3] *Vide* LETTER IX.

[4] These were corporations in the Middle Ages, the members of which were engaged in literary pursuits, either writing or printing books, as well as in painting. It was, in short, a guild of all artistic craftsmen.

Dear old Bernard,

A thousand thanks for the drawings you sent me.[2] I like especially the avenue of plane trees beside the sea with two women chatting in the foreground and some passers-by. I like too the woman under the apple-tree, the one with an umbrella; also the four drawings of nude women, especially the one washing herself, chiefly grey, with touches of black, white, yellow and brown. It's delightful.

Ah! Rembrandt . . . all admiration for Baudelaire apart, I venture to suggest that judging from those particular lines he had practically no idea of Rembrandt[3]: I found here the other day, and bought, a small engraving after Rembrandt, a study of a nude man, realistic and simple. He stands, leaning against a door or a pillar, in a dark interior, and a shaft of light from above illuminates his downcast face, and his mass of red hair. One is reminded of Degas by the real and animal-like feeling of the body. Have you ever, for example, *really* looked at the *Slaughtered Ox*,[4] the interior of a butcher's shop, in the Louvre? Of course you haven't and Baudelaire even less so.

It would be a distraction for me to spend a morning with you in the Dutch room. It's not something one can really put on paper, but in front of the pictures themselves I could point out to you the marvels and miracles which are the reason why—in the first place and most directly—I do not admire the primitives at all.

You see, I am not much of an eccentric: it's the calm, modelled perfection of a Greek statue, a peasant by Millet, a Dutch portrait, a nude woman by Courbet or Degas, which make many other things, from the primitives to the Japanese, seem to me like so much calligraphy. It interests me endlessly, but something complete, a perfection, makes the infinite tangible; and the enjoyment of something beautiful is like the moment of coïtus, a moment of infinity.

Have you, by chance, come across a painter called Vandermeer,[5] one of whose pictures is of a very beautiful, pregnant, Dutch lady. This strange painter's palette is made up of: *blue, lemon yellow, pearl grey, black and white*. His few pictures actually have all the richness

59

of a full palette, but the combination of lemon yellow, pale blue and pearl grey is as characteristic of him as black, white, grey and pink is of Velazquez.

I know of course that the works of Rembrandt and the other Dutch painters are widely scattered through museums and other collections, so it's not easy to form an opinion of them if one only knows the Louvre.

But actually it is Frenchmen like Charles Blanc,[6] Thoré,[7] Fromentin[8] and a few others, who have written more sensibly about this school than the Dutch themselves.

They hadn't much imagination or fantasy these Dutch painters, but they had plenty of taste and a knowledge of composition. They didn't paint Christ, or God, or anything of that sort—Rembrandt did of course, but he's *the only one* (and biblical subjects form but a relatively small part of his work),[9] he's the only one who, as an exception, painted Christs etc. . . . And anyway in his case they are not like the works of any other religious painter, they have a metaphysical magic.

Rembrandt also painted angels. He paints himself too, in old age, toothless, wrinkled and wearing a white cotton nightcap, primarily a picture from nature, looking at himself in a mirror. He's dreaming and dreaming and his brush begins again a portrait of himself, head and shoulders only, and the expression becomes more shattered and more shattering. He goes on dreaming, and I don't know how or why, but just as Socrates and Mahomet had a familiar spirit, so behind this old man, who resembles himself, Rembrandt paints a supernatural angel with a da Vinci smile.[10]

Here I am pointing out to you a painter who dreams and paints from imagination, and yet I began by explaining that one of the Dutch characteristics is that they don't invent, that they have no imagination or fantasy.

Am I illogical? No.

Rembrandt didn't invent anything, he knew this angel and this strange Christ, and *felt them there*.

Delacroix suggests Christ with the unexpected note of brilliant lemon yellow, this patch of light and colour acting in the picture with the same strange, unspeakable charm of a star in some corner of the heavens. Rembrandt works with tonal values in the same way as Delacroix works with colours.

And there's a big gap between the methods of Delacroix and Rembrandt and those of the other religious painters.

I will write again soon. This is just to thank you for your drawings which are giving me a lot of pleasure. I have just finished a portrait of a girl aged 12,[11] with brown eyes, black eyebrows and hair, greyish yellow skin, the background white heavily touched out with emerald green, her bodice blood-red with violet stripes, her skirt blue with large orange spots, a branch of pink oleander in her pretty little hand.

I'm absolutely worn out, so much so that I haven't even the head for writing any more. Till soon again: and once more many thanks.

Yours,
Vincent.

[1] *Vide Letters to Theo* No. 514, dated 29th July: this refers also to Bernard's drawings, and to Vincent's portrait of a young girl. This letter is written on a plain sheet of white paper measuring $8 \times 5\frac{1}{4}$ inches (20.5×13.2 cm.).

[2] Presumably the ones asked for in LETTER X.

[3] cf. LETTER XIII, Note 4.

[4] *Le Bœuf Écorché*, by Rembrandt, Louvre No. 2548, Hofstede de Groot catalogue No. 972. The picture shows an ox's carcass hanging in a butcher's shop.

[5] He means Vermeer van Delft: the picture in question seems to be the *Lady reading a Letter*, in the Rijksmuseum, Amsterdam.

[6] Charles Blanc (1813–82), an art critic: author of *'Grammaire des arts du dessin'* and editor of the vast *'Histoire des Peintres'*. His more famous brother, Louis, a historian and politician, fled from France after occupying a post in the provisional government of 1848, returned only in 1870 and wrote an account of the reign of Louis Philippe: *'Histoire de Dix Ans'*.

[7] Etienne Joseph Théophile Thoré, wrote under the pseudonym of W. Burger (1807–69). A provincial lawyer, also writer: he was one of the most active participants in the Revolution of 1848 and as a result was forced to flee the country. But he was pardoned under the General Amnesty. A great amateur of art and author of *'Guides en Belgique et en Hollande'*, *'Musées d'Amsterdam et la Haye'*, *'Trésors d'Art de la Grande Bretagne, exposés a Manchester en 1857'*, *'Notices sur Rembrandt'*.

[8] *Vide* LETTER VI, Note 9.

[9] A strange enough statement when it is remembered that Biblical subjects form probably one-fifth of Rembrandt's work.

[10] He is apparently referring here to the picture now in the museum at Cologne (Carstanjen Bequest), Hofstede de Groot catalogue No. 560.

[11] de la Faille No. 431; *vide Letters to Theo* Nos. 514, 516. This is the so-called MOUSMÉ.

Dear old Bernard,

You will, I am quite sure, admit that neither you nor I can have a complete idea of either Velazquez or Goya, either as men or as painters: for neither of us has ever seen Spain, their country, or the many fine things still left in the South. But, still, the little one does know is already something.

It goes without saying that, as for the people of the North, beginning with Rembrandt, it is highly desirable, when judging these painters, to know both their work in all its scope and also their country, and the rather intimate and concise history of the period and its ancient customs.

I insist that neither Baudelaire nor you have a sufficiently clear idea of Rembrandt.

So that in your case I can only advise you to spend a long time looking at both the major and minor Dutch painters before forming an opinion. It isn't merely a question of distinguishing between precious stones, but it's a question of choosing gems among gems. And there's a certain amount of paste among the diamonds.

Although I have been studying my national school for at least 20 years, I wouldn't even answer most questions about it for I've heard so much rubbish talked when the northern painters were under discussion.

So that my only answer to you is: Bah! have another and a better look, really it's well worth the trouble.

When, for example, I declare that the Ostade in the Louvre, *The Painter's Family*² (the man, his wife and about ten children) is infinitely worthy of study and reflection, like the *Peace of Münster* by Terborch, and when the paintings in the Louvre which I personally prefer and find the most exciting are often overlooked by artists, even by those who go to look at the Dutch School, then I am hardly surprised: for I know that my choice in that school is the result of a knowledge which most French people will never acquire.

But if, for example, you and I were to disagree, I should feel sure that eventually you would see that I was right.

What pains me so in the Louvre is to see their Rembrandts left to rot, and those idiotic curators allowed to ruin so many lovely pictures.

The unpleasant yellow tone of certain Rembrandts is the result of deterioration from dampness and other causes: there are cases I could point out to you. It's as difficult to say what was the real colour of Rembrandt as it is to give an accurate name to the grey of Velazquez. For want of something better one might as well call it "Rembrandt gold". And that's what one does, but it's pretty vague.

Coming as a foreigner to France, I, perhaps more than most French people, have felt Delacroix and Zola, for whom I have the most sincere, deep and unbounded admiration.

I already had a pretty complete idea of Rembrandt: Delacroix worked directly with colours, Rembrandt with tonal values—but in the end they are equals.

As painters of a society, a whole world, Zola and Balzac produce rare artistic emotions in those who enjoy them, just because they embrace the whole of the epoch which they are depicting.

Although Delacroix paints humanity, life in general, instead of an epoch, he is nevertheless a member of the same family of universal geniuses.

I am very pleased with the final paragraph of, I think, Silvestre,[3] who ended a masterly article thus: "Thus, almost with a smile, died Eugène Delacroix, a painter of noble stock; a sun was in his head and a storm in his heart; he could turn from warriors to saints, saints to lovers, lovers to tigers, and tigers to flowers."

Daumier is also a great genius.

Millet is another painter of a whole people and the world which it inhabits.

Perhaps these great geniuses are after all only madmen, and perhaps one must be mad oneself to have such boundless faith in and admiration for them.

If that were the case, I would prefer my madness to the rest of the world's sanity.

An indirect approach to Rembrandt is possibly the most direct road. So let's take Frans Hals. He never painted Christs, Adorations of the

Shepherds, Angels, Crucifixions or Resurrections: nor did he ever paint voluptuous, bestial, nude women.

He painted portraits: nothing, nothing but that.

Portraits of soldiers, gatherings of officers, portraits of magistrates assembled to settle the affairs of the Republic, portraits of matronly old ladies with pink or sallow skins, wearing white caps and dressed in black satin or wool, who discuss the budget of some orphanage or almshouse. He painted the portrait of many a good bourgeois surrounded by his family, husband, wife and children. He painted the tipsy drunkard, the haggish old fish-wife in gay mood, the pretty gypsy tart, babies in swaddling clothes, the dashing, fine-living gentleman with his moustache, boots and spurs. He painted himself too with his wife, young lovers seated on a grass bank in a garden the day after their wedding night. He painted hardened toughs and smiling urchins, musicians too and a great fat cook.

That's about as much as he knew; but still—it's worth Dante's Paradise, or Michelangelo or Raphael, or even the Greeks. It's as good as Zola, but healthier and more cheerful, though just as vital because his period was healthier and not so sad.

And now what about Rembrandt?

Well, he's just the same: he too was a portrait painter.

That's the healthy, broad, clear conception one must have from the start of these two equally great Dutchmen, before going into further detail. Having grasped this, the whole glorious Republic depicted by these two prolific portraitists, reconstructed with bold outlines, we are left with plenty of room for the landscapes, interiors, animal paintings, and philosophical subjects.

But follow carefully, I beg you, my sound reasoning which I am making a very special effort to present as simply as possible.

Get this master Frans Hals into your head, a painter of all kinds of portraits, the immortaliser of a whole vital and dazzling republic. Then get into your head the other no less great and universal master of portraiture from the Dutch Republic: Rembrandt Harmensz van Ryn, a large and very human figure, as healthy as Hals himself. After these comes a whole line of real pupils issuing directly from Rembrandt:

Vermeer van Delft, Fabritius, Nicholas Maes, Pieter de Hooch, Bol and some others merely influenced by him, Potter, Ruysdael, Ostade, and Terborch. I have mentioned Fabritius, of whom only two pictures are known, I've *left out* several good painters, and above all the paste among these diamonds; that paste is already familiar enough to the ordinary Frenchman.

Do you find me very incomprehensible my dear Bernard? I'm just trying now to make you see a great and simple thing: the depiction of humanity, or rather let us say of a whole republic, through the simple means of portraiture. That's really the first and most important point. If after that, where Rembrandt is concerned, we occasionally meet with mysticism, with Christs, with nude women, then it's very interesting but not by any means the principal thing. Let Baudelaire hold his tongue on such matters, his words may be sonorous but they're certainly empty![4]

Baudelaire is all right in his place as a modern poet, just as de Musset is another, but he'd better mind his own business as far as painting is concerned. I don't like your drawing *Lechery*[5] as much as the others. I like *The Tree*: it has dignity.

A handshake,

Yours,

Vincent.

¹ There is no means of dating this letter with certainty as it deals with a matter never mentioned in any letter to Theo. But it obviously belongs closely to LETTER XII and presumably precedes LETTER XIV. Moreover the curt reference at the end to two only of Bernard's drawings is in contrast to the effusive thanks at the beginning of LETTER XII and indicates that he has now had time to study them. Vincent often wrote two letters in the same day to Theo and it seems to me that quite possibly he spent the whole day thinking over Baudelaire's lines and wrote this present more serious letter either on the same evening or next day. This letter is written on a sheet of white paper measuring $10\frac{1}{2} \times 8\frac{1}{4}$ inches (27 $\times$ 21 cm.), ruled in a network of small squares.

² *Portrait de Famille* formerly called *La Famille d'A. von Ostade*, by Adriaen van Ostade; Louvre Dutch School catalogue, No. 2495.

³ Théophile Silvestre (1823–75), French journalist and *littérateur*. A violent Republican: appointed *commissaire* after the Revolution of 1848. For a time art critic on *Le Figaro*, a Paris daily paper. 1857–9 charged with a mission to inspect the museums and other fine art centres of Europe. He is the author of '*Histoire des artistes vivants, français et etrangers*' (1856); '*Les Artistes Français*' (1861); '*Eugène Delacroix*' (1864). He was a personal friend of Delacroix and Courbet.

⁴ Emile Bernard says: "All this was provoked by my quoting with admiration the lovely quatrain from Baudelaire's '*Phares*':
'Rembrandt triste hôpital tout rempli de murmures
Et d'un grand crucifix décoré seulement,
D'où la pierre en pleurs s'exhale des ordures
Et d'un rayon d'hiver traversé brusquement.' "
which might be translated as follows:
"Rembrandt—sad hospital filled full with murmurings, decorated only by an immense Crucifix, where the stone tearfully exhales filth and is rudely traversed by a ray of winter."
'*Les Phares*' is one of the poems included in the volume '*Les Fleurs du Mal*'. In it Baudelaire apostrophises various artists, Rubens, Leonardo, Rembrandt, Michelangelo, Puget, Watteau, Goya and Delacroix, drawing his moral about Art in the last verse:
"Car c'est vraiment, Seigneur, le meilleur témoignage
Que nous puissions donner de notre dignité
Que cet ardent sanglot qui roule d'âge en âge
Et vient mourir au bord de votre éternité."
"For, Lord, the best witness we can bear to our dignity is this burning sigh which echoes from age to age and finally dies away on the edge of your eternity."

⁵ *Lubricité*.

Dear old Bernard,

I see I have omitted to answer your question whether Gauguin is still at Pont-Aven. Yes, he is still there and if you were to write to him I'm sure he'd be pleased. He's staying there for the moment, though probably he'll join me here soon, that is as soon as we can get the money from somewhere or other for his fare.

This question of the Dutch painters which we were discussing recently seems to me not without interest. As far as concerns virility, originality, or some measure of naturalism, they are well worth study. But I must first talk to you about your own work, about two still lifes you have done and two portraits of your grandmother. Have you ever done anything better? Yet have you ever been more *yourself* and more of a person? I doubt it. A profound study of the first thing which came to hand, or the first person who came along, sufficed to produce *a real creation*. Do you know why I like these 3 or 4 studies so much? It's because they have something deliberate, sensible, something solid and self-assured. But you've never been closer to Rembrandt, my dear.

It was in the studio of Rembrandt that the matchless sphinx Vermeer van Delft learnt that exceedingly solid technique which has never been surpassed, and which we're burning to discover today. Of course, I realise that our discussions and our work centre round *colour*, whereas their concern was with *chiaroscuro* and *tonal values*.

But what's the importance of such differences when, after all, the only thing that matters is the force of one's expression?

At the moment then you're studying the methods of the Italian and the German primitives, the symbolic significance which may exist in the abstract and mystic line of the Italians. Carry on!

There's a story about Giotto which I like. There was a competition for painting some picture or other of the Virgin, and several designs were submitted to the artistic authorities at the time. One of these, signed Giotto, was simply an oval, a plain egg-shape.² The authorities, intrigued—and trusting—entrusted the Virgin in question to Giotto.

I wonder if it's true: but anyway it's a good tale.

However let's get back to Daumier[3] and your grandmother.

When are you again going to let us see some sketches as solid as those? Soon, I urge you; though I don't at all despise your researches into the effect of opposing movements in lines—I hope I myself am not indifferent to direct contrasts of lines and forms. The trouble is you see, my dear Bernard, that Giotto and Cimabue like Holbein and Van Dyck lived in an obeliscal—excuse the word—scaffolded society built up architecturally, in which each individual was a stone and all the stones held together and made up the monumental social structure. And when the socialists start—which they are still pretty far from doing—to construct their social order logically we shall, I am sure, see a recrudescence of that society. But now, you know, we're in the middle of *laisser-aller* and anarchy.

And we artists who love order and symmetry have shut ourselves off to work and define *one sole object*.

Puvis[4] knows that all right and when he, so wise and so just—leaving for a while his Elysian Fields—set out to penetrate as a friend into the intimacy of our time he produced a fine portrait: a benign old man in his well-lit blue room, reading a novel with a yellow paper cover—beside him a glass of water with a water-colour brush and a rose in it. He also painted a fashionable lady, the sort the Goncourts[5] depicted.

Now the Dutch painted things just as they are, apparently without intellectual intervention, just as Courbet[6] painted lovely nude women. They painted portraits, landscapes, still lifes. One can be a lot stupider than that and make worse mistakes.

When we don't know what to do, my dear Bernard, then we should follow them: even if only to avoid wasting our rare mental force in sterile metaphysical meditation, which doesn't straighten out the chaos, for the very chaos only exists because no human vessel can hold it.

But we can—and that's what the Dutch did, they were infernally cunning for people with a system—we can paint a fragment of the chaos: a horse, a portrait, your grandmother, apples, a landscape.

Why do you say that Degas[7] hasn't much physical passion? Degas

69

lives like some small lawyer and doesn't like women, realising that if he did like them and spent his time embracing them, his mind would suffer and he would lose his grasp over painting.

Degas' painting is virile and rightly impersonal, because privately he's resigned to being nothing but a small lawyer with a horror of the gay life. He looks at stronger human animals than himself, coupling up and embracing, and paints them well, just because he doesn't try to do it himself.

Rubens! There's a handsome man for you and a great lover. Courbet too. But their health could withstand drinking, eating and making love.

But as for you, my dear Bernard, I've been warning you all this spring: eat sensibly and do your military exercises well, don't make too much love, in fact the less of this you do the more spunk you'll have to put in your painting.

Balzac, that fine, powerful artist, was right when he said that comparative chastity merely strengthened the modern artist.

The Dutch were *married men and begot children:* it's a fine thing to do, and so absolutely natural.

One swallow doesn't make a summer. I'm not saying that your new studies of Breton women aren't virile and solid: I haven't seen them, so how could I? But I have seen something thoroughly virile, the portrait of your grandmother and the still life. Still I'm rather doubtful, from your drawings, whether the new studies will have the same force, to the extent of being really virile.

These sketches I mentioned first of all you see are the first swallow of your artistic summer.

If we really want to put all our strength into our work we must sometimes make up our minds to love rather less, and, according to our temperament, live like soldiers or hermits.

The Dutch, to mention them again, had habits and a life which were peaceful and well-ordered.

Delacroix—there's another for you!: "I discovered the way to paint," he wrote, "when I had neither teeth nor breath left". Someone who actually saw him paint said: "When Delacroix paints it is like a lion

70

PLATE 24

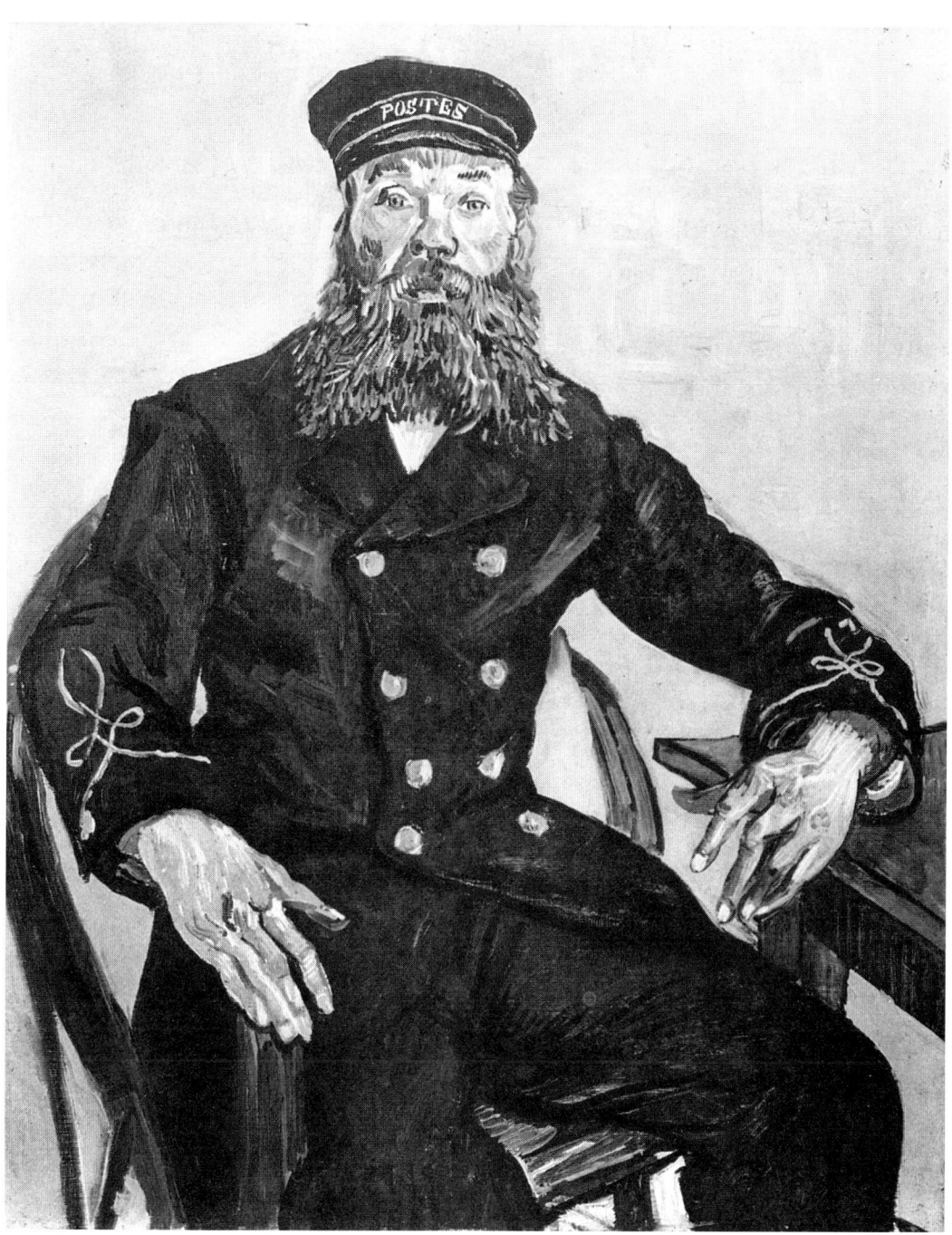

THE POSTMAN ROULIN

devouring his prey". He didn't do much love-making and never had serious love affairs, so as not to waste the precious time which ought to be devoted to work.

If in this letter, which is more incoherent in appearance, considered as a whole and in relation to your letters, and especially to our friendship, than I had meant it to be—if, I say, from its contents you gather that I feel a certain uneasiness—at any rate solicitude—about your health, in view of the coming grave trial it will have to face during your military service, then this letter will not have been in vain. I know that the study of the Dutch painters can do you nothing but good, for their work is so virile, so dashing, so healthy. Continence suits me personally, and it enables our weak impressionable artists' brains to put all their energy into the creation of pictures. For reflection, calculation and fatigue use up a great deal of mental energy.

Why strive to pour out all one's creative seed where the well-fed professional *maquereau* or everyday client can satisfy the prostitute's genitalia more effectively, especially as she is [more] submissive in this case than us anyway.

Besides the prostitute in question has more my sympathy than my compassion.

An exile, an outcast from society, like you and me, artists, she is our friend, our sister.

And being an outcast, like us, gives her a form of independence which is not without its advantages, taken as a whole. So don't let's deceive ourselves into thinking we would be doing her a service by reinstating her in society: a pretty impracticable project and fatal to her.

I have just done a portrait of a postman[8] or rather two portraits even.[9]

A socratic type, and none the less so for being something of a drinker and having as a result a high colour. His wife recently had a child, the good man is simply beaming with satisfaction. He is terribly republican, *like old Tanguy*.[10] A damn good subject to treat like a Daumier, eh! He stiffened too much while he was posing, that is why I painted him twice, the second time at a single sitting. The canvas is white, background blue verging on white, and in the face the whole gamut of broken tones, yellows, greens, violets, pinks, reds. His uniform Prussian blue, with yellow details.

Write to me soon if you feel like it. I'm very busy and haven't yet found time to sketch figures.

A handshake.

Yours,

Vincent.

PS. Cézanne is just the same sort of bourgeois married man as the old Dutch painters; if there's plenty of kick in his work it's because he doesn't waste his substance in riotous living.

---

[1] The reference to the two portraits of Roulin, the postman, links this letter with *Letters to Theo* Nos. 516, 517, 518, which were written in the first days of August. In addition there is the question of Bernard's arrival at Pont-Aven, which occurred at the beginning of August. Bernard himself confirms this: he left for Pont-Aven on receipt of this letter. He was then on his annual walking tour in Brittany. This letter is written on two sheets of paper: one ruled in small squares measuring $10\frac{1}{2} \times 8\frac{1}{4}$ inches (27 × 21 cm.), the other plain white measuring $8 \times 5\frac{1}{4}$ inches (20.5 × 13.2 cm.).

[2] He inserts here a drawing of an oval.

³ Honoré Daumier (1808–79), French caricaturist, draughtsman and painter.

⁴ Pierre Puvis de Chavannes (1824–98), a classicistic painter, for a while a pupil of Delacroix; the most important decorative painter of the latter half of the century. He was responsible for frescoes in the Museum at Amiens, the Panthéon and the Sorbonne in Paris. A friend of the Impressionist group, but not a member.

⁵ Edmond (1822–96) and Jules (1830–70) de Goncourt, two brothers, novelists and authors of the famous Goncourt *'Journal'* in which they attempted to record as objectively as possible for posterity all that they saw and heard around them.

⁶ Gustave Courbet (1819–77), one of the leaders of the realist school of French painters.

⁷ Hilaire-Germain-Edgar Degas (1834–1917), originally associated with the Impressionist group at their first exhibitions.

⁸ Roulin, postman at Arles who became a faithful friend to Vincent. *Vide Letters to Theo* Nos. 516, 517, 518. *Vide* Plate 24.

⁹ Probably de la Faille Nos. 432 and 434.

¹⁰ "Le Père Tanguy" as he was called, a colour merchant from whom Vincent bought much of his materials, and whose shop was in the Rue Clauzel. He is one of the most picturesque and sympathetic figures of the period. He was born in 1825, in Brittany, began life as a plasterer, married a woman who kept a pork-butcher's shop and finally entered the employ of the Ouest railway. In 1860 he moved to Paris, left the railway company and took a job as colour grinder for a firm in the Rue Clauzel. Very soon he began a colour business of his own, not opening a shop but grinding the colours himself and peddling them in the environs of Paris. His colours must have been of very good quality—Monet, Renoir, Cézanne and others of the Impressionists all bought from him. Tanguy gave them very long credit and accepted pictures in payment: these he stacked up in his room. In the Commune of 1871 his sympathies were ardently revolutionary and he ended up doing two years in a prison ship. In 1875 he opened a shop of his own in the Rue Clauzel which was immediately patronised by all his old customers, and he continued the old system of allowing payment in pictures: his shop was one of the main artistic meeting-places of Paris and Vincent was a frequent visitor. In fact, it was at Tanguy's that the only recorded meeting between van Gogh and Cézanne took place. Van Gogh painted Tanguy (de la Faille Nos. 363 and 364) showing him seated in front of some of the Japanese prints which he sold as a side line. Tanguy died in 1894.
I have compiled this note from an article on Julien Tanguy by Emile Bernard, in the *Mercure de France*, of December 16th, 1908.

My dear Bernard,

I want to do figures, figures and more figures. It's stronger than I
am this race of bipeds, from the baby to Socrates, from the woman
with raven black hair and white skin to the woman with yellow hair
and a brick-red face baked by the sun.[2]

Meanwhile I am doing mostly other things.

Thanks for your letter. This time I am writing in great haste, and
absolutely worn out.

I am very pleased you have gone to join Gauguin.[3]

All the same I have a new figure study, which is absolutely a continuation of certain studies of heads I did in Holland. I showed them
to you one day with a large picture of that period, *The Potato
Eaters*[4]: I wish you could see the new one.[5] It's still a study, but colour
plays such an important part that a black and white drawing wouldn't
give you any impression of it.

I wanted to send you a very large and careful drawing of it. But
then it was really something quite different, accurate though it was.
For the colour again suggests the burning heat of harvest-time in the
south, right in the middle of the dog-days; without that it's quite
another picture.

I like to think you and Gauguin would understand it: but the others
will find it ugly all right!

You know what peasants are like, how much of the wild beast there
is about the genuine article.

I have also a *Men Unloading a Sand-Barge*. That is to say there
are two boats, purplish pink in emerald green water, with grey sand,
barrows, planks and a little chap in blue and yellow. All that seen from
a quay above, in other words a bird's eye view. No sky: it's only a
study, or rather a very rough sketch, done in the teeth of the *mistral*.[6]
Further, I am attempting some dusty thistles with a big swarm of
butterflies fluttering around them.[7]

The full summer sun here is lovely. It beats down on one's head
and I am sure it makes one crazy. But as I was that before, anyhow,

I can revel in it.

I am thinking of decorating my studio with half-a-dozen pictures of *Sunflowers*[8]: a decoration in which chrome yellow, crude or broken, shall blaze forth against various backgrounds of *blue*, ranging from the very palest emerald up to *royal blue* and framed with thin strips of wood painted *orange*.

The sort of effect of Gothic stained glass windows.

Ah! dear friends, we crazy ones get pleasure through our eyes all right, don't we?

Unfortunately Nature takes her toll of the beasts, our bodies are disgusting and frequently a heavy charge. But ever since Giotto, who suffered a lot, it has been thus.

And, all the same, what pleasure he took in his sight, what a smile, the toothless smile of that old lion Rembrandt wearing his white cotton nightcap and with his palette in his hand.

I would love to be able to come and spend a few days at Pont-Aven: however, I seek consolation by looking at the sunflowers.

A cordial handshake: and till soon again.

Vincent.

[1] I have been unable to study the original of this letter as it is missing from the collection in the possession of the Baroness de Goldschmidt-Rothschild. The connections between this letter and Nos. 523 and 524 of the *Letters to Theo* confirm this date.

[2] He must be referring to Roulin, his wife and children, and the girl, aged 12, whose portrait he refers to in LETTER XII.

[3] Bernard moved to Pont-Aven at the beginning of August: *vide Letters to Theo* No. 523, and LETTER XIV, Note 1.

[4] A subject painted twice by van Gogh (he also made a lithograph) during his stay at Nuenen (1883–5) with his family. Nuenen is a small village not far from Eindhoven in the southernmost part of Brabant where his father was Pastor. *Vide* de la Faille Nos. 78 and 82.

[5] Probably the portrait of Patience Escalier (de la Faille Nos. 443, 444), "a species of human being with a hoe, at one time cowherd of the Camargue, now gardener at a house in the Crau". In *Letters to Theo* No. 520, he writes: "The colour of this peasant portrait is not so black as in THE POTATO EATERS of Nuenen . . ."

[6] de la Faille No. 449; a sketch of this picture is in *Letters to Theo* No. 524.

[7] This painting is unknown, but it is probably the same as the one referred to in LETTER XVIII; *Vide* LETTER XVIII, Note 10.

[8] cf. LETTER XXII: this disposes finally of Gauguin's assertion that van Gogh never thought of doing sunflowers until he, Gauguin, arrived in Arles.

Dear old Bernard,

Thank you for your letter; but I am rather surprised to hear you say "Do Gauguin's portrait? Why, that's impossible!"[2] Why is it impossible? That's all nonsense. But I won't insist and so we definitely won't mention this exchange any more. So: on his side then Gauguin has not even thought of doing your portrait. What sort of portrait painters are these? Living together all this while, you haven't even managed to pose for each other, and now you will be separating without having done each other's portrait! Well, I won't insist. And, as I have just said, the exchange is off.

One day then I hope to do a portrait of you and of Gauguin myself —as soon as we are all together, which is bound to happen.

One day now I am going to do the portrait of that second lieutenant of the Zouaves I told you about,[3] he will be leaving soon for Africa.

Why haven't you replied to my questions about your plans for your military service?

Now let's talk for a moment about your idea of coming to spend the winter here in Arles. I have installed myself here specially in such a way that I can, if necessary, house somebody. But then supposing Gauguin comes! He hasn't yet definitely refused: and even if I could put you up, I cannot see how you could feed yourself properly on less than 3 francs a day, and it would be safer to say 4 francs.

Naturally, if we were hard up, we could have lots of meals cheaply in the studio; it's always possible of course to economise in that way. Life here, as I told you, comes a little more expensive than at Pont-Aven. I think you are paying only 2·50 frs. a day, aren't you, board and lodging included?

But supposing the subject which interests you most, the interior of brothels—which is indeed an excellent subject—could not be had for nothing here!

Wait until you have got your uniform: soldiers—here and elsewhere—can get a lot of things for nothing!

Take my case, for instance, it's true I have just done that study of

77

the *Night Café*[4]; but then, though it is a shady place, and one does from time to time see a tart at table with her man, I have not yet been able to do a real brothel, as I told you, *just because to make something serious of it would cost me more money than I have for such purposes*. So I refrain from starting till I know my purse is fat enough to be able to bring it off satisfactorily. Mind you, I am not saying we won't go and have a glass of beer in such places; we'll make friends there and be able to work partly from imagination, partly with a model. And if we want to I don't say it would be impossible to bring something off: but at present, anyhow, I for one am *not in the least in a hurry*. One's plans so often fall through, however well worked out, whereas by relying on chance and working from day to day with no fixed programme, one ends by producing a lot of surprising things.

So I cannot possibly urge you to come down here for the express purpose—an excellent purpose no doubt—of painting brothels. As I said before, once you're a soldier you'll have plenty of opportunity for that, and in your own interest you would probably do better to wait till you have your uniform. But, my dear Bernard, there is one thing I want to say to you clearly and at once: go and spend your time in Africa. You will adore the South, and it will make a great artist of you. Even Gauguin owes his mastery to the South.[5] I myself have been seeing the stronger light of these parts now for months and months and the result of this experience is that the people who stand up best, from the point of view of colour, are Delacroix and Monticelli; yet these are the painters who today are wrongly accused of being pure romantics and having exaggerated powers of imagination. In short, you see, the South which was so dryly painted by Gérôme and Fromentin is from now on essentially a landscape whose intimate charm can only be expressed by a real use of colour.

I hope you will write to me again soon. I don't dare risk persuading anyone to come down here. If anyone comes of his own accord, well that's his own look-out: but as for *recommending* it, that I won't ever do. Personally I am staying here, and naturally I would be very pleased if you can come to spend the winter. A handshake.

Yours, *Vincent*.

78

PLATE 25

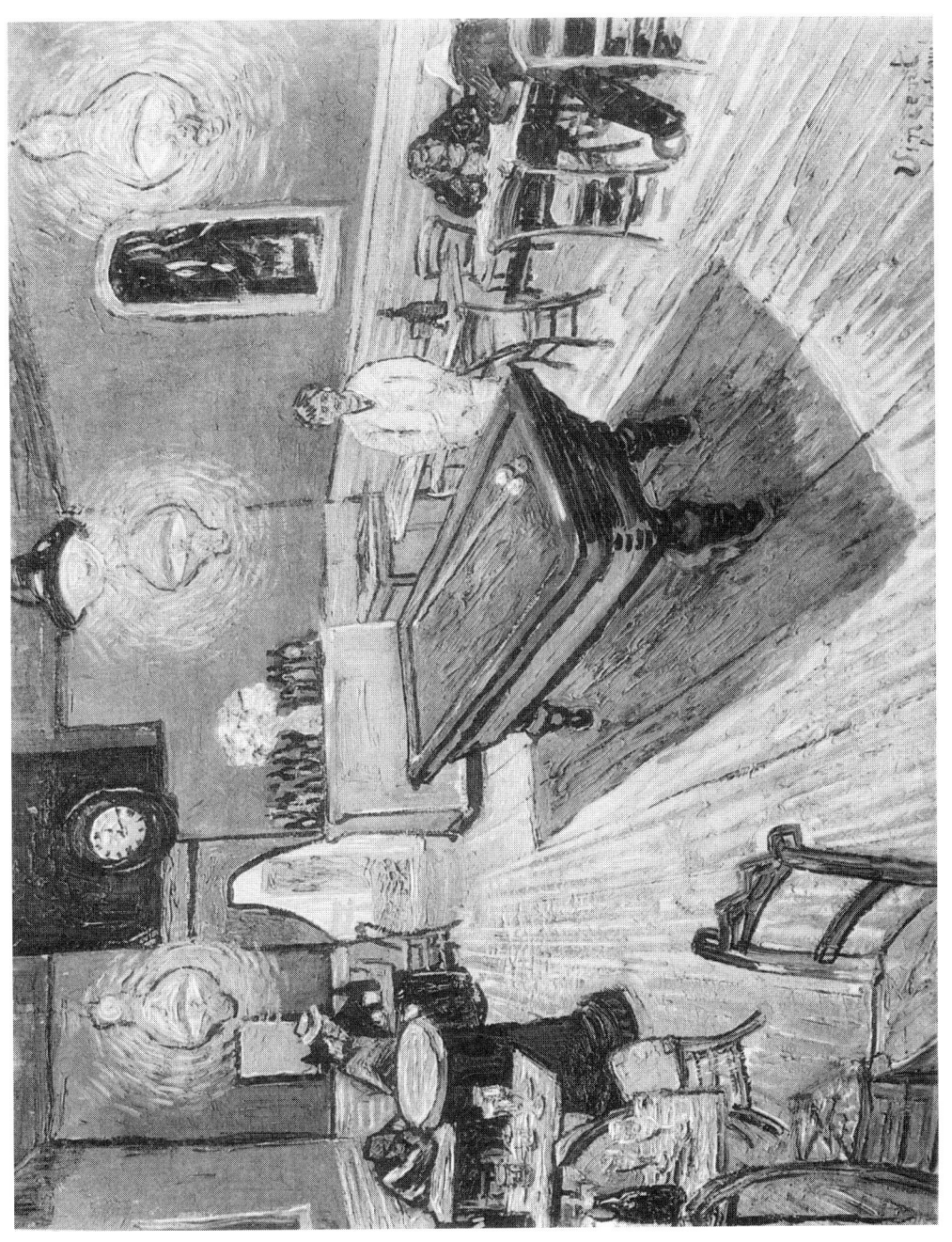

THE NIGHT CAFÉ

¹ *Letters to Theo* No. 533 (dated 8th September) states that the NIGHT CAFÉ is finished. In Letter 535 he says he has written to Bernard and Gauguin asking them to do each other's portrait and exchange them with him. In Letter 538 he says he has had a "very kind" letter from Bernard; in Letter 539 he says that Bernard is too frightened to do Gauguin's portrait. The present letter was probably written, therefore, about the same time as it is the reply. This letter is written on a sheet of white paper measuring $8 \times 5\frac{1}{4}$ inches (20.5×13.3 cm.) and ruled with a network of squares.

² *Vide Letters to Theo* No. 539.

³ *Vide* LETTER VII; the picture referred to is probably de la Faille No. 473. *Vide* LETTER VIII, Note 9.

⁴ Plate 25; de la Faille No. 463.

⁵ A reference obviously to Gauguin's stay in Martinique.

XVII

Dear old Bernard,

Just a word to thank you a lot for your drawings: I think they betray too much haste and I prefer the two drawings of prostitutes; but there's an idea behind all of them. I have a great deal of work to do right now, because the weather is marvellous and I must profit by the fine days, which are all too short.

There is no altering the price I gave you, 3 francs for food alone, on top of which there would be . . . well just whatever there would be. But whatever Gauguin told you about the cost down here is, I am sure, correct. But I imagine you are on the verge of departing to do your military service; I wish I could induce your father to provide what you need to strengthen you first, so that your work doesn't suffer. He really ought to fork out and give you something reasonable during the time between now and your departure.

I keep on writing the same thing to you: if you go to Africa you will work there and you will find just the sort of scenery you ought to see if you are ever fully to develop your painting and your colour sense. But I'm afraid it will be at the expense of your poor body if your father doesn't get you fit enough before this African venture to resist anæmia or the weakening effects of dysentery, which come from a lack of strengthening food.

It's hardly possible to get up one's strength over there and when one is going into a hot climate I don't by any means suggest one should fatten oneself up first, but I do say that one should pay attention to what one eats for quite a while beforehand: I can't get away from it, having been so well here on this diet, because the heat of Africa is quite another thing to the heat of Arles.

Either you will come out of this trial much stronger, strong enough to stand a whole artistic career—or else a broken man.

Anyhow I would love you to come here, and if Gauguin comes too all we shall have to regret is the fact that it is winter and not the best time of year. More and more I'm coming to believe that food has something to do with our powers of thought and picture-making: I, for one, have no success with my work if my stomach is bothering me. I think if your father were quietly to accept your pictures and give you a generous advance on them he would probably lose less in the long run than by doing it some other way. In the south one's senses wake up, the hand becomes more agile, the eye more alert and the brain more clear, but on one condition: that it's not all spoilt by the weakening effect of dysentery or something else.

That's what makes me believe that anyone who is really interested in his work as an artist will find his creative powers developing in the south: but you must look to your blood and everything else.

You will say perhaps that I am boring you with all this: that you will go to brothels and that you don't care a damn about the rest. Well that depends; but anyway it doesn't alter what I have to say. Art is long and life is short, and we must be patient while we are trying to sell our skin dearly. I wish I were your age and could go off knowing what I know to do my military service in Africa; but I'd get myself a better body than I have, to be sure.

If Gauguin and I are here together, as is probable, we will certainly do all we can to save you expense, but then, on his side, your father ought to do all he can too, he ought to have confidence in us and realise that we're not just trying to get money out of him unnecessarily.[2] If one is to produce good work one needs to eat well, to be well housed, to have one's fling from time to time, and to smoke one's pipe and drink one's coffee in peace.

I don't say that nothing else is important, each person must suit himself about that: but what I do say is that this system seems to me better than many others.

A hearty handshake,
Yours,
Vincent.

¹ This letter was probably written about 25th September. *Letters to Theo* No. 543 (headed "September") reads: "As I wrote to Bernard that I thought he could not live in the south for less than 3.50 or 4 francs a day for board and lodging alone . . ." Also: "I think that Bernard would find what he wants here, but his father would really have to be a little more generous to him." Bernard was still with Gauguin at Pont-Aven. This letter is written on a sheet of white paper measuring $8\frac{1}{4} \times 5\frac{1}{2}$ inches (21 × 13.5 cm.) ruled in a network of squares.

² Vincent had had a row with Bernard's father at Asnières in 1887 because he refused to listen to Vincent's advice about Bernard's future.

XVIII

Dear old Bernard,

This time you deserve more praise for the little drawing of two Breton women in your letter than for the six others, because the little one has great style. I myself am behindhand with the drawings, having been absolutely taken up during the present marvellous weather with canvases 30 square, which are very tiring and are eventually to be used to decorate my house.[2]

You will already have received my letter setting out seriously my reasons for advising you to try and persuade your father, supposing he pays your fare to Arles, to give you a little more latitude in your purse.

I think you would pay him back in work, and in this way you would be longer with Gauguin and your departure to do your military service would mark the beginning of a fine artistic campaign. If your father had a son who looked for unrefined gold and found it in pebbles or on the pavement he certainly would not despise such a talent. Yet, in my opinion, your talent is just as good as that.

Your father, though he might regret that they were not beautiful pieces of shining new gold, already coined into *louis*,[3] would certainly collect whatever you found and only sell it for a reasonable price.

He ought to do the same thing with your pictures and drawings, which commercially are as rare and as valuable as precious stones or rare metals.

And that's absolutely true.

It's as difficult to make a picture as it is to discover a diamond, be it large or small. But whereas everyone knows the value of a golden *louis* or a fine pearl, unfortunately those people who know the value of pictures and believe in them are rare. Still such people do exist.

Anyway there's nothing better to do than sit and wait patiently, even if one has to wait a very long time.

On your side you must think over carefully what I have told you of the cost of living here and whether you really want to join Gauguin and me in Arles. Tell your father that, given a little more money, you would be able to paint much better pictures.

The idea of a sort of freemasonry among painters doesn't please me very much. I profoundly despise rules, institutions etc. I am out for something more than mere dogmas, which, far from arranging matters, simply give rise to endless disputes. They are a sign of decadence. Since a union of painters doesn't yet exist, except as a very vague though very broad idea, we had better wait quietly and let what will happen.

It will be much better if the idea crystallises naturally, the more one talks about it the less this will happen. If you want to help it on you only have to keep in with Gauguin and me. It's already under way, don't let's discuss it further. If it is ever to come to anything it will not be through enormous discussions, but through a series of calm, carefully considered actions.

As for the matter of exchanges,[4] it is just because I have read so much in your letters about Laval,[5] Moret[6] and the other young man[7] that I am so anxious to meet them. But I haven't five studies which are dry, I'll have to add at least two rather more serious attempts at pictures: a self portrait and a landscape with the full wrath of the howling *mistral*.[8]

Then I should have a study of a small garden with flowers of many colours,[9] a study of thistles which are grey with dust[10] and finally a still life of old peasant shoes:[11] last of all a little landscape, only a stretch of country, nothing at all really.[12] If they don't like any of these studies, or if one or the other isn't satisfied, all you have to do is to keep those which are chosen and return to me with the exchanges those not wanted. There's no hurry, and in this matter of exchanges it is only right that each should try to give something good.

If exposing it to the sun tomorrow will dry it sufficiently to be rolled up, I will add an outdoor study of *Men Unloading Sand*,[13] also a draft for and attempt at a picture, which shows a more mature force of will.

I cannot send you yet another version of my *Night Café*[14] because it hasn't even been begun, but I certainly will do one for you.

Once again it is preferable that each of us should try and exchange something good, rather than something done in too much of a hurry.

The artistic gentleman in the letter[15] who looks like me—do you think it's me or someone else? The face certainly suggests that it is me, but in the first place I always smoke a pipe and secondly I have the utmost horror of sitting like that on precipitous rocks overhanging the sea, it makes me giddy. So if that's supposed to be a portrait of me I must protest at the above-mentioned inaccuracies.

I am terribly absorbed in the decoration of my house,[16] I can't help feeling that it is rather to your taste, although it's obviously very different from what you do. But still you did once talk to me about a series of pictures, one representing *Flowers*, another *Trees*, another *The Fields*. Well I have the *Poets' Garden*[17] (2 canvases) (among the sketches you will find the first version of it, taken from a smaller painted study which is already at my brother's).[18] Then there is the *Starry Night*,[19] the *Vineyard*,[20] the *Furrows*,[21] then the view of the house, which might be called *The Street*.[22] So that involuntarily there is a certain sequence.

Well I am very curious to see your studies of Pont-Aven. From you I want something which is really worked on. Anyhow, that can always be arranged, because I admire your talent so much that bit by bit I hope to make a small collection of your work.

For a long time I have been very struck by the fact that the Japanese artists often used to exchange works among themselves. That proves that they liked and supported each others' work, and that a certain harmony existed among them: the relationship between them was evidently, and quite naturally, brotherly, they didn't live a life of intrigue. The more we can copy them in this respect the better for us. It appears too that the Japanese earned very little money and lived like simple workmen. I have the reproduction (published by Bing) *A Single Blade of Grass*. How *conscientious*! One day you will see it. A hearty handshake.

Yours,
Vincent.

85

[1] *Letters to Theo* No. 544 mentions the receipt of a letter from Bernard in which he "says once more that he wants to come here (Arles)", and proposes, on behalf of himself and three others, to make an exchange. Letter 543 reads: "It is no more easy, I am convinced, to make a good picture than it is to find a diamond or a pearl, it means trouble . . ." The present letter presumably follows closely on LETTER XVII and would be the "answer" referred to in Letter 544.
This letter is written on a sheet of white paper measuring $8\frac{1}{4} \times 5\frac{1}{2}$ inches (21 × 13.5 cm.) ruled in a network of squares.

[2] *Vide* LETTER XV, Note 8; also LETTER XXII.

[3] A French gold coin first minted in the time of Louis XIII: it was then worth 24 *livres*—a coin later replaced by the franc. At this time a *louis d'or* was a 20-franc piece.

[4] Bernard had written to Vincent, proposing that he should exchange one of his canvases with each of the four artists mentioned—Bernard, Laval, Moret and Chamaillard.

[5] Charles Laval, a painter of the Pont-Aven group: he sailed with Gauguin to Panama in 1887 and engaged too, as workman, in the digging of the Panama Canal.

[6] Another of Gauguin's and Bernard's intimate friends at Pont-Aven.

[7] de Chamaillard, also an intimate of the Pont-Aven group: *vide Letters to Theo* No. 544.

[8] This description is too vague for the pictures to be identifiable.

[9] Drs. Scherjon and Gruyter suggest that this may be de la Faille No. 578: more probably it is de la Faille Nos. 429 or 430.

[10] Perhaps de la Faille No. 447: cf. LETTER XV, Note 7.

[11] Probably de la Faille No. 461: alternatively No. 607.

[12] Drs. Scherjon and Gruyter suggest that this may be de la Faille No. 576.

[13] This may be de la Faille No. 438; or it may be No. 439, the picture described in LETTER XV, which is more probable.

[14] *Vide* LETTER XVI: de la Faille No. 463; cf. LETTER XIX.

[15] Bernard writes: "The allusion is to a caricature by Gauguin representing Vincent seated on the tip of a rock, busy painting the sun."

[16] cf. Note 2.

[17] Probably de la Faille No. 468; *vide Letters to Theo* No. 537, dated 17th September, 1888: the second canvas is unidentified. In *Letters to Theo* No. 546 (headed "October") he mentions having two pictures of THE POET'S GARDEN framed.

[18] Probably de la Faille No. 428: there is a sketch of this painting in *Letters to Theo* No. 508, of July 1888.

[19] Perhaps de la Faille No. 474.

[20] Perhaps de la Faille No. 475.

[21] Drs. Scherjon and Gruyter suggest de la Faille No. 574.

[22] Plate 9; de la Faille No. 464.

Dear old Bernard,

Almost simultaneously with the departure of my own sketches, packets arrived from you and Gauguin. I'm in fine form now, and it warmed my heart properly to see your two faces again.[2] Your portrait, you know, I like enormously. I like everything you do however, as you know, and probably no one *before* me was ever *so* enthusiastic as I am about your work.

I urge you strongly to concentrate on portraits, do as many of them as you can and don't give up. Later on we'll have to get at the public with portraits, that, in my opinion is the way the future lies. But don't let us get lost in hypotheses now.

As I have started dealing out thanks, I will continue by thanking you for the group of little sketches entitled *At the Brothel!*[3] Bravo! The woman washing herself and the one saying "There isn't another like me for satisfying a man!" seem to me the best; the others are too mocking and above all too loose, they haven't enough body, there's not enough construction. Not that it matters, for there's something new and interesting even in the less good ones. To the brothel! yes that's where one must go, and I assure you that I for one am almost jealous of the grand opportunity you will have by going there in uniform: they'll go crazy the good little women.

The poem, at the end, is really fine, it stands on its own feet better than many of your figures. You say what you mean, and what you say you believe, very well and sonorously.

Write to me when you will be in Paris. As I wrote you a thousand times already my night café isn't a brothel[4]: it's a café where the night prowlers cease to be night prowlers, because they flop down at a table and spend the whole night thus, without prowling at all. Occasionally a tart brings her man in. But coming in one evening I did catch sight of a little group of a *maquereau* and his tart making it up after a row. The woman was being proud and indifferent, the man was wheedling. I set myself to paint it for you from memory on a little canvas of 4 or 6. So if you are leaving soon I will send it to Paris:

but if you are staying on let me know and I'll send it to Pont-Aven; it wasn't dry enough to be sent with the others. I don't want to sign this sketch as I never work from memory. You'll find some colour to please you, but once again it's a study done specially for you, and I would rather not have done it.

In spite of their colour, which was perfect, I had ruthlessly to destroy an important canvas—*Christ with the Angel in Gethsemane*[5] and another of the *Poet against a Starry Sky*,[6] because the form had not been studied from the model first, an absolute necessity in such cases. If you don't like the study I am sending you in exchange, look at it a little longer. I had the devil of a job doing it with the *mistral* raging (like the red and green study too). And although it is not as fluently painted as the *Old Mill*,[7] it is finer and more intimate. It's got nothing to do with Impressionism, but what does that matter anyway. What I do is the result of abandoning myself to nature, without thinking of this or that. It goes without saying that if you would prefer another study from the lot, instead of the *Men Unloading Sand*,[8] you can take it, and blot out my dedication if someone else wants it. But I think the first one will please you once you have looked at it a little longer.

It's perfect if Laval, Moret and the other man[9] want to exchange with me. For my part I would be content if they would each do me their own portrait.

You know Bernard I think if I want to do sketches in brothels it will cost me more money than I have, because I am no longer young and not sufficient of a lady's man to get them to pose for me for nothing. And I can't work without a model. I'm not saying I don't turn my back on nature completely when I'm working a sketch up into a picture, arranging the colours, enlarging or simplifying: but as far as the forms are concerned I'm terrified of getting away from the possible, of not being accurate.

Later perhaps, after another 10 years study, things may be different: but honestly I am so intrigued by what is possible, by what really exists, that I haven't either enough desire or courage to seek after the ideal as it might result from my abstract studies.

Others seem to have more feeling for abstract studies than I do, indeed you may be among the number, Gauguin too . . . myself too perhaps when I am old.

Meanwhile I devour nature ceaselessly. I exaggerate, sometimes I make changes in the subject; but still I don't invent the whole picture, on the contrary I find it already there, it's a question of picking out what one wants from nature.

You will probably find these studies ugly. I don't know. In any case neither you, nor I, nor any of us need make an exchange unwillingly. My brother writes that Anquetin is back in Paris, I wonder what he has been doing. When you see him give him kind messages from me.

My house will seem more inhabited now that I shall see the portraits in it. How happy I would be to see you here in person this winter! It's true the journey is rather costly. But can't you risk getting that expense back from your work? Winter in the north makes work very difficult! Here too perhaps: I haven't really had any experience of it as yet, but we'll see. But it's damned helpful to a better understanding of the Japanese if one has seen the south, where so much more of one's life is spent out of doors.

Then the strange haughtiness and nobility of some of the landscape round here would keep you busy.

In the *Red Sunset*[10] the sun should be imagined higher up, outside the picture, just about *on the level of the frame.* An hour to an hour and a half before sundown things on the earth still have their natural colour, as in the painting. But later on the blue and violet make them look blacker, as soon as the sun's rays become more horizontal. Many thanks again for your packet which really warmed my heart, and a hearty handshake in thought. Write to me the date of your departure so that I shall know when you will be in Paris: your Paris address is still 5 Avenue Beaulieu, isn't it?

Yours,
Vincent.

¹ This letter is later than LETTER XVIII, judging merely from the reference to the exchanges. In addition, there is the reference to Bernard's and Gauguin's portraits arriving, and also the fact that the NIGHT CAFÉ has been painted from memory: *Vide Letters to Theo* No. 548. This letter is written on a sheet of white paper measuring $8\frac{1}{4} \times 5\frac{1}{2}$ inches (21×13.5 cm.), ruled in a network of small squares.

² *Vide Letters to Theo* No. 545: *Vide* LETTER XVI.

³ A series of "10 drawings with a daring poem" by Bernard: *vide Letters to Theo* No. 545.

⁴ *Vide* LETTER XVI.

⁵ This incident is presumably the one referred to in *Letters to Theo* No. 505. He does not necessarily mean that he has just destroyed it. Letter 505 seems to have been written in July.

⁶ The "poet" in question was a Belgian artist with whom Vincent had made friends in Arles. He is described as "a young man with a look of Dante". He posed to Vincent for the picture de la Faille No. 462. *Vide Letters to Theo* Nos. 520 and 531.

⁷ de la Faille No. 550.

⁸ *Vide* LETTER XVIII.

⁹ *Vide* LETTER XVIII, Note 7.

¹⁰ Probably the same picture as the one described in LETTER VII: Plate 22.

My dear friend Bernard,

The other day my brother wrote me that you were going to see my pictures. So I know then you are back, and I am very pleased that you should have thought of going to see what I have done.

On my side I am very anxious to know what you have brought back from Pont-Aven.

I haven't really got much of a head for correspondence,² but I feel a great gap by no longer being in touch with everything that Gauguin, you and the others are doing.

Still, I must be patient.

I have another dozen studies here, which will probably be more to your taste than those of this summer, which my brother will have shown you.

Among these studies there is an *Entrance to a Quarry*³: pale lilac rocks against a reddish soil, as in certain Japanese drawings. In design and in the use of large planes of colour it has quite a lot in common with what you are doing at Pont-Aven.

I have been more master of myself in these last studies, because my condition has greatly improved. Thus there is also a canvas of 30 with ploughed fields of a broken lilac shade and a background of mountains which rise up to the top of the picture⁴: just nothing but plain earth and rocks, with a thistle and some dried grass in one corner, and also a little chap in violet and yellow.

That will prove to you, I hope, that I am no longer so weak.

My God, it's a mighty tricky bit of country this, everything about it is difficult to do, that is if one is really to get at its inner character so that it's not merely something vaguely experienced, but the true soil of Provence. And to manage that one has to work hard, then naturally it becomes a bit abstract; for it's a question of giving the sun and the blue sky their full force and brilliance and yet not omitting the fine aroma of wild thyme which pervades the hard-baked, often melancholy, landscape.

However, it's the olive trees here, old man, which would be your meat. I haven't had much luck with them myself this year; but I'll come back to them, at least I intend to. They are quite silver in an orange or purplish landscape under a large white sun. Indeed, I have seen things by other painters, as well as by myself, which didn't get it at all. There is primarily something of Corot in this silvery grey, and that particularly is what no one has yet done, though many artists have been successful with apple-trees, for example, or willows.

Thus there are relatively few pictures of vineyards, which actually have a great and changing beauty.

So you see there's still plenty for me to get my teeth into here.

There's something I am very sorry to have missed at the Exposition,[5] that is the collection of dwellings of all the races. I think it's either Garnier[6] or Viollet-le-Duc[7] who has organised it. So could you, since you have seen it, give me an impression of it, and especially a sketch with the colours of the primitive Egyptian dwelling. I imagine it's very simple, probably a plain cube on a terrace[8]—but I would also like to know its colouring.

In an article I read that it was blue, red and yellow. Did you notice that? Please don't forget to let me know. And don't get it mixed with the Persian or the Moroccan, there are probably others more or less of the same sort, but still they won't be exactly that.

As for myself, however, the most admirable thing I know, as far as architecture is concerned, is the cottage with a moss-covered thatch roof and a well-blackened hearth. So you see I'm very hard to please.

In one of the illustrated papers I saw a sketch of ancient Mexican dwellings, they too seem to have been primitive and very beautiful. Oh, if only one knew about those times and could paint the people of those days who lived in such dwellings—that would be just as beautiful as Millet: I don't say as far as colour is concerned, but in character, as something significant, as something in which one has a solid faith.

Now what about your military service? Are you going? I hope you will go and see my pictures again when I send the autumn studies in November; and if possible let me know what you have brought back from Brittany, for I am very anxious to know what you yourself think are your best things.

I will write again soon then.

I am working on a big canvas of a *Ravine*,[9] a subject very like that study of yours with a yellow tree which I still have; two masses of mighty solid rock between which flows a thin stream of water, and at the end of the ravine a third mountain, which blocks it.

Such subjects have a fine melancholy, and moreover it's fun working in rather savage places, where one has to wedge the easel in between the stones to prevent everything being blown over by the wind.

A handshake,

Yours,

Vincent.

---

[1] In Letter No. 18, dated 4th October 1889, of the volume *Lettres de Théo van Gogh à son Frère Vincent* there occurs the sentence: "Bernard is supposed to be coming to-morrow to see your pictures, after that I am to go out to him to see

what he has brought back." In Letter No. 20, dated 16th November 1889, Theo writes: "I went this week to Bernard's . . ."

In addition there are the references to the paintings ENTRANCE TO A QUARRY and PLOUGHED FIELD WITH MOUNTAINS IN THE BACKGROUND which are mentioned in *Letters to Theo* No. 610, in which, moreover, the present letter was enclosed: "I send you enclosed a line for Isaacson, Bernard and Gauguin. There is no hurry about sending it on to them, the first time they come to see you will do."

There has been a break of a whole year between this letter and the last one. Gauguin arrived in Arles at the end of October 1888; on December 23rd occurred the dreadful ear episode and after that Vincent was in hospital at Arles. In May 1889 he entered St. Rémy asylum: at the beginning of July he was seized with a fit and it was not until August that he began to work again, and even then not outside his room; *vide Letters to Theo* No. 605: ". . . it is nearly two months since I have been in the open air."

This letter is written on a sheet of white paper measuring $8 \times 5\frac{1}{4}$ inches (20.5 × 13 cm.), ruled in a network of little squares.

2 *Vide Letters to Theo* No. 509: "I would like to write to . . . and Bernard, but writing does not always go well . . ."; and again: "How I would like to see what Gauguin and Bernard have brought."

3 de la Faille No. 744.

4 de la Faille No. 641.

5 The Paris Exposition of 1889 for which the Eiffel Tower was erected.

6 Charles Garnier (1825–98), French architect: his greatest work was the Paris Opera House.

7 Eugène-Emmanuel Viollet-le-Duc (1814–79), French architect and writer on archæology. At the time of the Second Empire he was responsible for the restoration of several mediæval buildings, notably the citadel of Carcassonne and the Château of Pierrefonds, near Compiègne. As he had been dead ten years when the Exposition opened there seems little possibility that he could have been responsible for the section Vincent is referring to.

8 "*un bloc carré sur une terrasse.*"

9 de la Faille Nos. 661 and 662. In *Letters to Theo* No. 610, he writes: "I have a sterner study than the previous one of the mountains. A very wild ravine where a small stream winds its way along its bed of rocks." This was written in the middle of October.

My dear friend Bernard,

Thank you for your letter, and especially for the photographs, which give me an idea of your work.

My brother, by the way, wrote to me about it the other day, saying he very much liked the harmonious colours and a certain nobility in many of the figures.[2]

Now in *The Adoration of the Magi* I find the landscape too delightful to venture on a criticism, but nevertheless it is going too far beyond the bounds of possibility to imagine a delivery in such circumstances, in the middle of the road and the mother in the act of prayer instead of giving suck: then there are those fat ecclesiastical toads who have fallen to their knees as though in a fit of epilepsy, God knows how or why they should be there! I don't think it's rational myself. Because personally I love things that are real, things that are possible, that is however if I am capable of a spiritual thrill, and that is why I bow before that sketch which is powerful enough to make even a Millet tremble—the one of peasants carrying back to the farm a calf just born in the fields. That, my friend, all people have felt from France to America. Are you now going to follow that up with a revival of mediæval tapestries? Is it really a sincere conviction? *Surely not*: you can do better than that, and you know that what you must strive for is the possible, the logical, the real, even if you do have to forget somewhat the Baudelairean aspects of Paris. How I prefer Daumier to that fellow!

An *Annunciation*, of what? I see figures of angels—elegant ones, certainly—a terrace with two cypresses, which I like a lot; there's plenty of air, plenty of light in it . . . but then, once the first impression is past, I ask myself if it is a mystification, the characters mean nothing to me any more.

But it's enough if you understand that I am longing to see from you more things like the picture of yours that Gauguin has, the Breton women walking in the meadows,[3] so beautifully ordered, so naïvely distinguished in its colouring. And now you exchange that for what is—must I say the word—artificial and affected.

PLATE 26

FACSIMILE FROM LETTER XXI

Last year you did a picture—according to what Gauguin told me—which I imagine to be somewhat as follows[4]: on the grass, which fills the foreground, lies stretched full length the figure of a girl in a blue or white dress; behind her the edge of a wood of beech trees, the ground covered with red leaves which have fallen, the tree-trunks grey-green giving the effect of vertical stripes.

The hair is, I suppose, a note of colour in the shade demanded as a complementary to the white dress; black if the dress is white, orange if it is blue. So I said to myself what a simple subject, and how well he achieves elegance with nothing.

Gauguin told me of another subject, simply three trees, an effect of orange foliage against a blue sky[5]; but still very carefully drawn, and deliberately divided into planes of strong contrasting colours—bravo!

But when I compare such things with that nightmare of a *Christ in the Garden of Olives* I am sad indeed; so by the present letter I command you, upbraiding you with all the force of my lungs, to become once more your own self.

The *Christ Carrying the Cross* is appalling. Do you think there's any harmony between the patches of colour in that? I won't forgive you orthodoxy—orthodoxy indeed!—in the composition.

When Gauguin was in Arles,[6] as you know, I once or twice allowed myself to turn to abstraction, as in the *Woman Rocking a Cradle*,[7] or the *Woman Reading a Novel*,[8] black in a yellow library; and at that time abstraction seemed to me to offer a charming path. But it's an enchanted territory, old man, and one quickly finds oneself up against a wall.

I don't say that after a manly lifetime of research, or hand to hand battles with nature, one might not risk it; but for my part I don't want to bother my head with such things. The whole year I have slaved away at nature, hardly giving a thought either to Impressionism or anything else. However, once again I let myself go reaching for stars too big, once more a catastrophe, and now I have had enough.

So at the moment I am working among the olive trees, seeking after different effects with a grey sky against yellow soil, and a green-black note in the foliage; in another the soil and the foliage are purplish against a yellow sky; then there's one with red ochre soil and greeny pink sky. These interest me far more than all the abstractions mentioned above.

If I haven't written for a long while[9] it is because what with having to wrestle with my illness and calm my head I had but little desire for discussion—and I found danger in these abstractions. If one goes on working quietly the fine subjects will come along of their own accord; above all it is really a question of sinking oneself anew in reality with no preconceived plan and none of the Parisian prejudices. I am more-over very displeased with this year's work; but perhaps it will prove a solid basis for the next one. I have absorbed as completely as possible the atmosphere of the little mountains and the olive groves: we'll see what happens. I don't want anything more than a few sods of earth, some sprouting wheat, an olive grove, a cypress—the latter not by any means easy to do.

I can't understand why you, who like and study the primitives, appear not to know Giotto. Gauguin and I saw a tiny panel by him at Montpellier,[10] the death of some good holy woman. The expression of pain and ecstasy in it are so utterly human that, 19th century though one may be, one feels oneself there—it is as though one were present—so strongly does one share the emotion.

If I were actually to see your pictures I believe that nevertheless I would be carried away by the colour, but you also talk of portraits you have done which have cost you much work: that's what will be good and where you will have been yourself.

Here's the description of a canvas in front of me at this moment. A view of the park of the asylum where I am[11]: on the right a grey walk, and a side of the building. Some flowerless rose-bushes, on the left a stretch of the park, red ochre, the soil parched by the sun, covered with fallen pine-needles. This edge of the park is planted with large pine-trees, the trunks and branches being of red ochre, the foliage green darkened by a tinge of black. These tall trees are outlined against an evening sky striped violet on yellow, which higher up shades off into pink and then into green. A wall—more red ochre—shuts out

98

PLATE 27

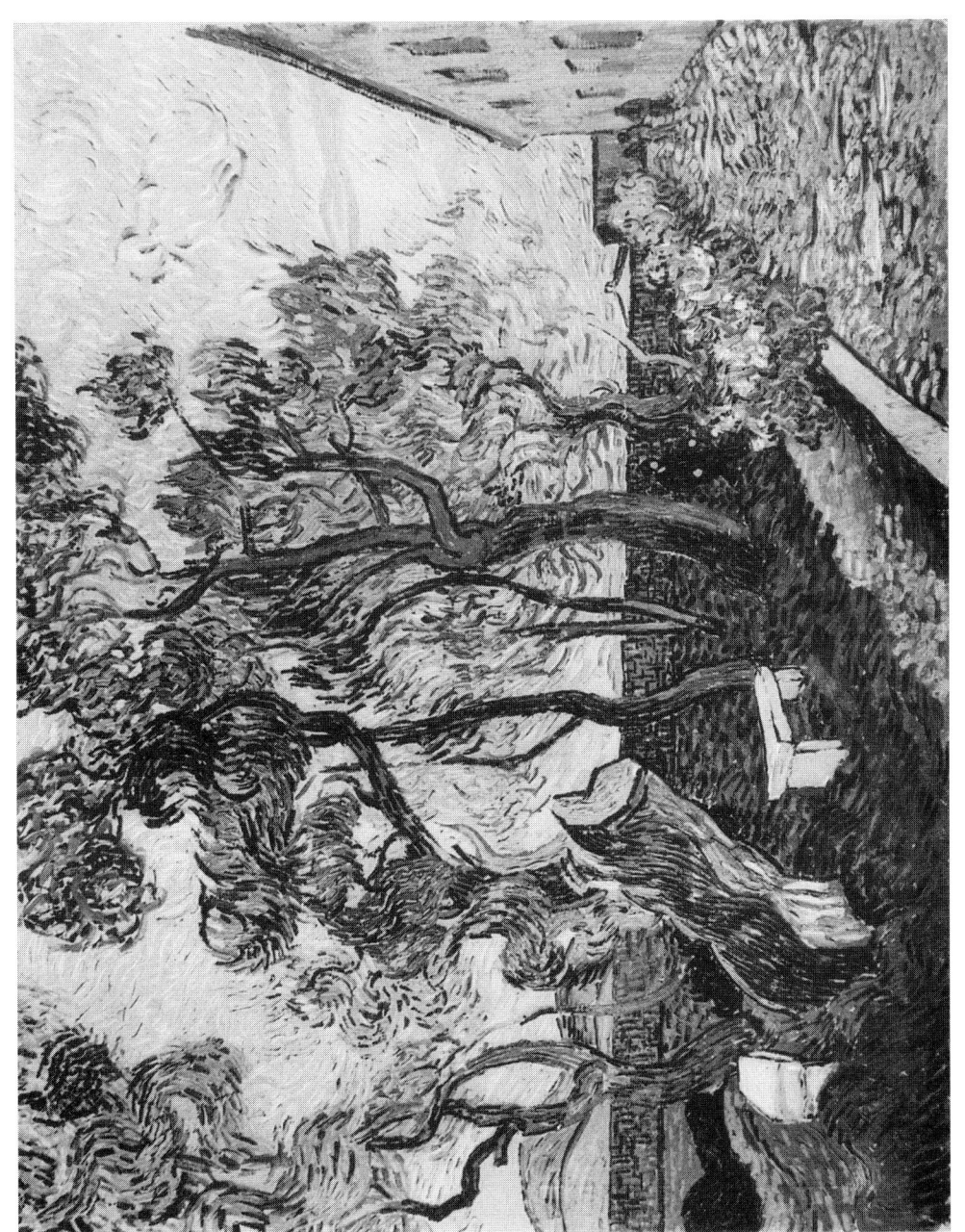

THE GARDEN OF THE ASYLUM AT SAINT-RÉMY

the view, or rather all of it except one hill which is violet and yellow ochre. The nearest tree is merely a large trunk which has been struck by lightning and then sawn off. But a side-branch shoots up very high and then tumbles back in an avalanche of dark green pine-needles. This sombre giant, proud in his distress, is contrasted—to treat them as living beings—with the pallid smile of a last rose on the fading bush right opposite him. Beneath the trees are empty stone seats, gloomy box-trees, and a reflection of the sky—yellow—in a puddle left after the rainstorm. A sunbeam, the last ray of light, raises the deep ochre almost to orange. Here and there small black figures wander about among the tree trunks.

You will realise that this combination of red ochre, green saddened by grey, and the use of heavy black outlines produces something of the sensation of anguish, the so-called *noir-rouge*, from which certain of my companions in misfortune frequently suffer. Moreover the effect of the great tree struck down by lightning and the sickly greeny pink smile of the last flower of autumn merely serve to heighten this idea.

Another canvas shows the sun rising over a field of young wheat[12]: a rushing series of lines, furrows rising high on the canvas towards a wall and a row of lilac hills. The field is violet and yellow-green. The white sun is encircled with a great yellow halo. There, in contrast to the other one, I have tried to express calmness, a great peace.

I am telling you about these two canvases, especially about the first one, in order to impress on you the fact that there are other means of attempting to convey an impression of anguish without making straight for the historic Garden of Gethsemane; that to convey something gentle and consoling it is not necessary to portray the figures of the Sermon on the Mount.

It is undoubtedly wise and just to be moved by the Bible: but the realities of today have so taken hold of us, that, even when attempting abstractly to reconstruct ancient times in our thoughts, our meditations are broken into by the minor events of our daily life and we are brought back forcibly by our own experiences into the world of personal sensations—joy, boredom, suffering, anger and laughter.

99

The Bible! The Bible! Millet, having been brought up on it from infancy, did nothing but read that book. Yet he never once, or practically never, painted a biblical picture. Corot painted a *Mount of Olives*, with Christ and the evening star, it's sublime: one can feel Homer, Aeschylus, Sophocles in his work, sometimes even the Gospel as well; yet how unobtrusive and with particular consciousness always of the possible feelings of today, which are common to all of us. But, you will say, what of Delacroix? Well, yes!

Delacroix—but then you would have to *study* all over again, yes *study* history, before fitting things into their places like that.

So I'm afraid, old man, your biblical pictures aren't a success[13]: there aren't many people who make a mistake like that, and mistake it is; but the result of it will, I am convinced, be magnificent. Sometimes it is by making a mistake that one finds the right road. Go and make up for it by painting your garden, just as it is—or anything else you like. Anyway it's a good thing to look for distinction, nobility in figures, and your studies do represent an effort, therefore they haven't been a waste of time. Being able to divide a canvas into a complicated series of large planes, finding lines and forms which make contrasts, that's technique, tricks of cooking[14] if you like, but still it's a sign that you are more a master of your profession, and that's always a good thing.

However hateful painting may be, and however burdensome at a time such as this, he who has chosen the profession and goes through with it zealously is being solidly faithful to his duty. Society at times makes our existence painful, hence our impotence and the imperfections of our work. Even Gauguin himself suffers much from it too, I think, and cannot find how to develop himself, although it's in him to do it. Myself I am suffering from an absolute lack of models. On the other hand there are lovely landscapes round here. I have just done 5 canvases of 30, olive groves. And I am staying on here because my health is improving a great deal. What I am doing is hard and dry, but that is because I am trying to get back into form through solid work, and because I am afraid that abstraction will merely weaken me.

Have you seen a study of mine with a little reaper, a yellow wheat-field and a yellow sun? It's not successful, but still in it I have tackled

PLATE 28

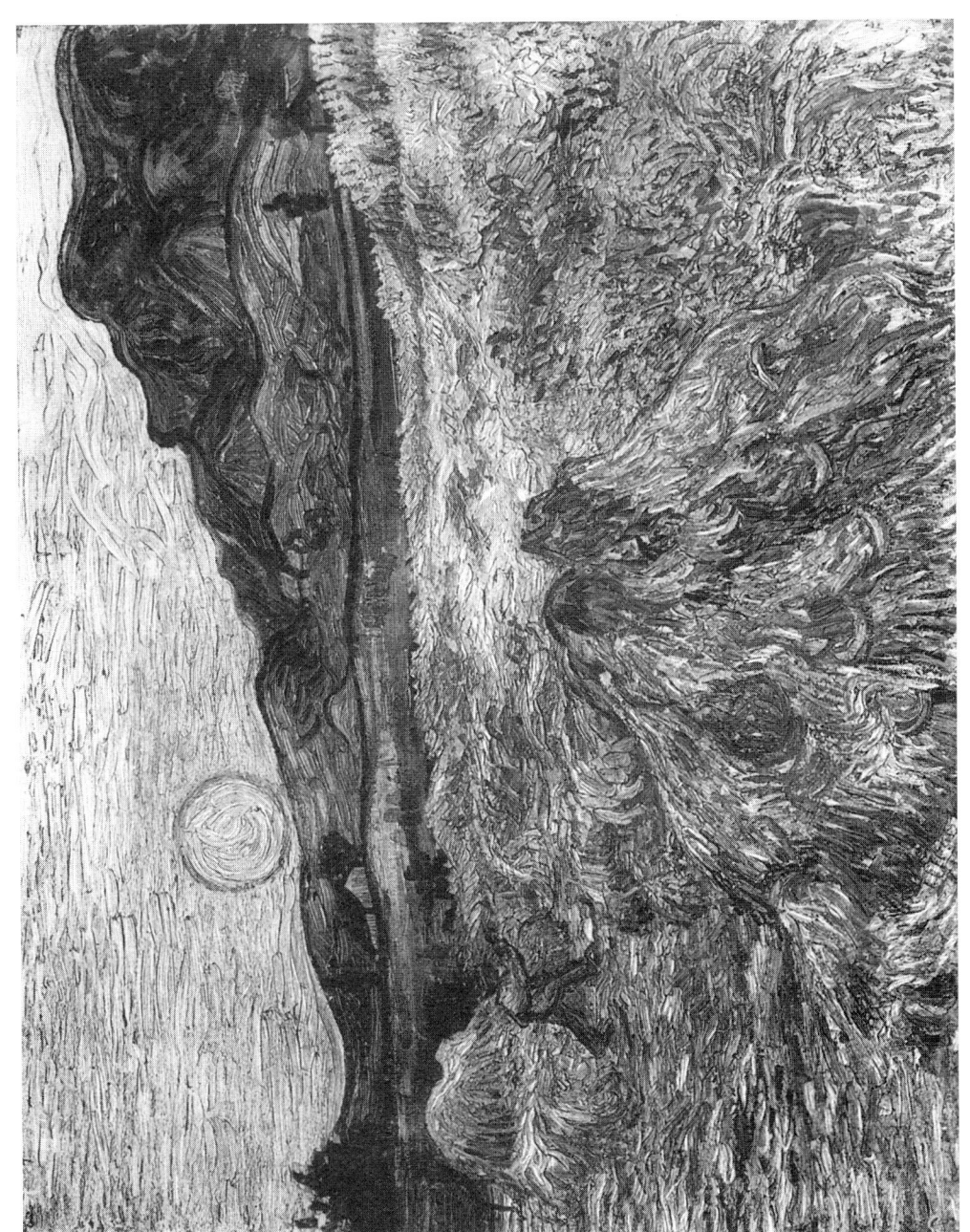

A REAPER AT WORK IN A WHEATFIELD AT SAINT-RÉMY

that devilish problem of yellows again. I mean the one with a heavy impasto done on the spot, not the duplicate with hatchings, the effect of which is weaker.[15] I wanted to do the first one entirely in sulphur.

I would still have many things to say to you, but if I write today it is because my head is rather steadier, previously I have been afraid of getting worked up before being cured. A very cordial handshake in thought for you, as well as for Anquetin and my other friends if you see any of them.

Believe me,

Yours,

Vincent.

PS. I don't need to tell you how sorry I am for your sake, and your father's, that he didn't agree to your coming to spend the winter with Gauguin. The latter wrote to me that for reasons of health your military service has been put off for another year. Many thanks, all the same, for the description of the Egyptian dwelling. I would still have liked to know whether it was larger or smaller than a present-day cottage; as well as its proportions in relation to the human figure. Still it was primarily about the colouring that I asked for information.

¹ *Letters to Theo* No. 614 (headed "November") reads: "Bernard also has written to me . . . I am not an admirer of Gauguin's *Christ in the Garden of Olives* for example . . . And then as for Bernard's, he promises me a photograph of it. I don't know, but I fear that his biblical compositions will make me want something different. . . .

"Our friend Bernard has probably never seen an olive tree. Now he avoids getting the least idea of the possible, or of the reality of things."

Letters to Theo No. 615 reads: "I have worked this month in the olive groves, because they have maddened me with their Christs in the Garden, with nothing really observed. Of course with me there is no question of doing anything from the Bible—and I have written to Bernard and Gauguin too, that I considered that to think, not to dream, was our duty, so that I was astonished, looking at their work, that they let themselves go like that. For Bernard has sent me photos from his canvases."

This letter is written on a sheet of white paper measuring $10\frac{1}{2} \times 8\frac{1}{4}$ inches (27×21 cm.) and ruled in a network of squares.

² Letter 20, dated 16th November 1889, in the volume of *Lettres de Théo van Gogh à son Frère Vincent*.

³ Bernard notes: "The canvas in question is called *Breton Women in the Meadows* and I wrote about it in the *Mercure de France* in my article *The History of the so-called School of Pont-Aven*: it was this picture which had such an influence on Gauguin's technique and provoked the row. He got it from me in 1888 in exchange for one of his own pictures of the same size, and took it with him to Arles where Vincent saw it and made a copy of it." The row in question arose from the fact that Gauguin denied being influenced by Bernard. *Vide A Note on Emile Bernard* in the present volume; also LETTER XXIII; also *Letters to Theo* No. 557.

⁴ Bernard notes: "The exactitude of this description shows to what extent Gauguin had absorbed the picture. It was painted in 1888 and was later in the collection of M. Amédée Schuffenecker." Van Gogh accompanies this description with two sketches in the text: Plate 26. The girl was Emile Bernard's sister.

⁵ Formerly in the collection of M. Eugène Bloch. *Vide* Plate 26.

⁶ From the end of October until 24th December 1888.

⁷ de la Faille Nos. 504, 505, 506, 507, 508.

From *Letters to Theo* No. 573 (dated 23rd January 1889) we learn: "I have in hand the portrait of Roulin's wife, which I was working on before I was ill." He repeated it four times after this as we learn from Letters 574 (dated 28th January 1889), 575, 576, 578 and 582.

102

[8] de la Faille No. 497; *vide Letters to Theo* No. 562, written at the end of November 1888. When van Gogh talks of "abstraction" he means simply painting without a model.

[9] Not for a month, apparently.

[10] Montpellier, a famous university town some 45 miles to the west of Arles. The picture referred to is probably No. 70 in the catalogue of the Montpellier Museum, namely *The Death and Assumption of the Virgin*, attributed now to the School of Giotto.

[11] Plate 27; de la Faille No. 659 or 660; *vide Letters to Theo* Nos. 618 and 619, both of which date from mid-December 1889; by then two versions of this subject existed.

[12] Possibly de la Faille No. 720. *Letters to Theo* No. 617, written in December, mentioned: ". . . the canvas for the Vingtistes, which I sent off yesterday; the field of corn with the sunrise."
The Vingtistes—more often written simply Les XX—were a group of 20 independent and advanced Belgian painters. From 1884–94 they had an annual exhibition in Brussels at which they invited 20 outside painters to take part. The secretary was Octave Maus: among those who exhibited were Cézanne, Monet, Renoir, van Gogh, Sickert, Sargent, Toulouse-Lautrec and Whistler.

[13] Bernard notes: "Vincent, who was a Protestant, had a special grudge against my spiritual conception of religious subjects as detached from their historical context, seizing merely on the very heart of the sensation; this is a thoroughly Catholic conception in which the thought prevailed over the facts."

[14] *"des trucs . . . de la cuisine."*

[15] Plate 28. Probably de la Faille Nos. 617 and 618; *vide Letters to Theo* No. 597: "The latest begun is the WHEATFIELD, in which there is a little reaper and a big sun. The canvas is all yellow except for the wall and the background of violet-tinted hills. The canvas, which is almost the same in subject, is different in colouring . . ."
In *Letters to Theo* No. 608 (written in September) we read: "At present as for the REAPER—first I thought that the large-size duplicate that I am sending you was not bad—but after, when the days of *mistral* and rain came, I preferred the canvas done from nature . . ."

XXII

Amongst his personal correspondence Emile Bernard also found the following letter from VAN GOGH *to* GAUGUIN.

[ARLES: MID-OCTOBER 1888][1]

My dear Gauguin,

Thank you for your letter and especially for your promise to come as soon as the 20th. Obviously the thing you mention[2] won't exactly contribute to the pleasure of your train journey, and it is only right that you should put it off until you can manage it without trouble.[3] But apart from that, I almost envy you the journey, for you will pass through miles and miles of varying countryside in all its autumnal splendour.

There is still present in my memory the emotion produced by my own journey last winter from Paris to Arles.[4] How I watched to see whether it wasn't something like Japan! Childish, wasn't it?

I wrote you the other day, you remember, that my sight was strangely tired. Well, having rested for two days and a half, I have taken up work again, though I haven't yet dared to go out of doors. Continuing the decoration I have done a canvas of 30, my bedroom with the white wood furniture which you know.[5]

Well, I enjoyed immensely doing this plain interior, it's as simple as a Seurat; flat tones crudely brushed on, and with a heavy impasto: the walls pale lilac, the floor a faded broken red, the chairs and the bed chrome yellow, the pillows and sheets a very pale lemony green, the quilt blood red, the washstand orange, the basin blue, the window green. I wanted to express a feeling of *perfect rest*, you see, by means of all these various tones among which there is no white at all, except for a small note within the black frame of the mirror (so as to make a fourth pair of complementaries).

Anyhow you will see it with the other things and we will talk about it, because often I hardly know what I am doing, working almost as in a trance.

It's beginning to turn cold, particularly those days when the *mistral* is blowing.

104

PLATE 29

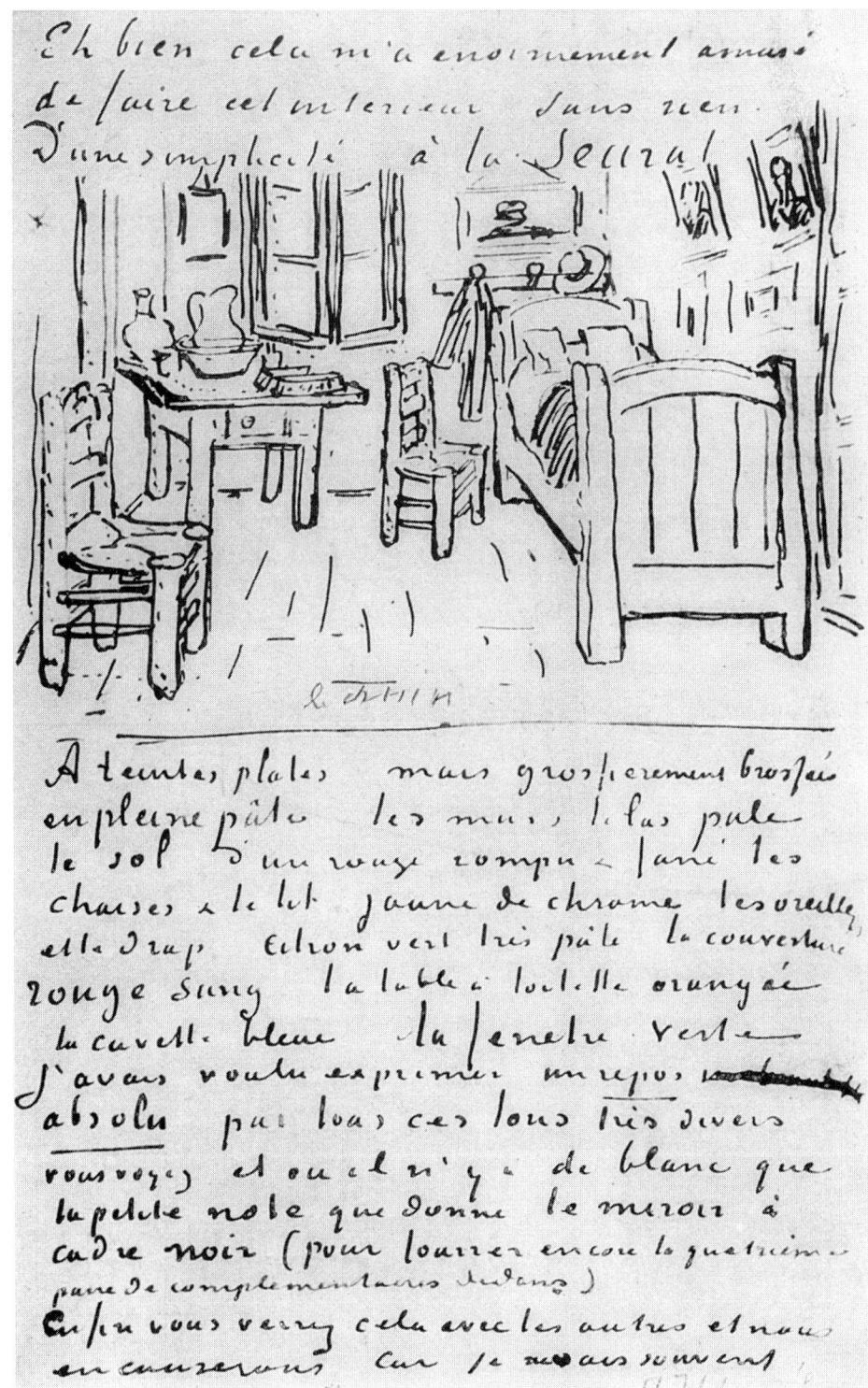

FACSIMILE FROM LETTER XXII

PLATE 30

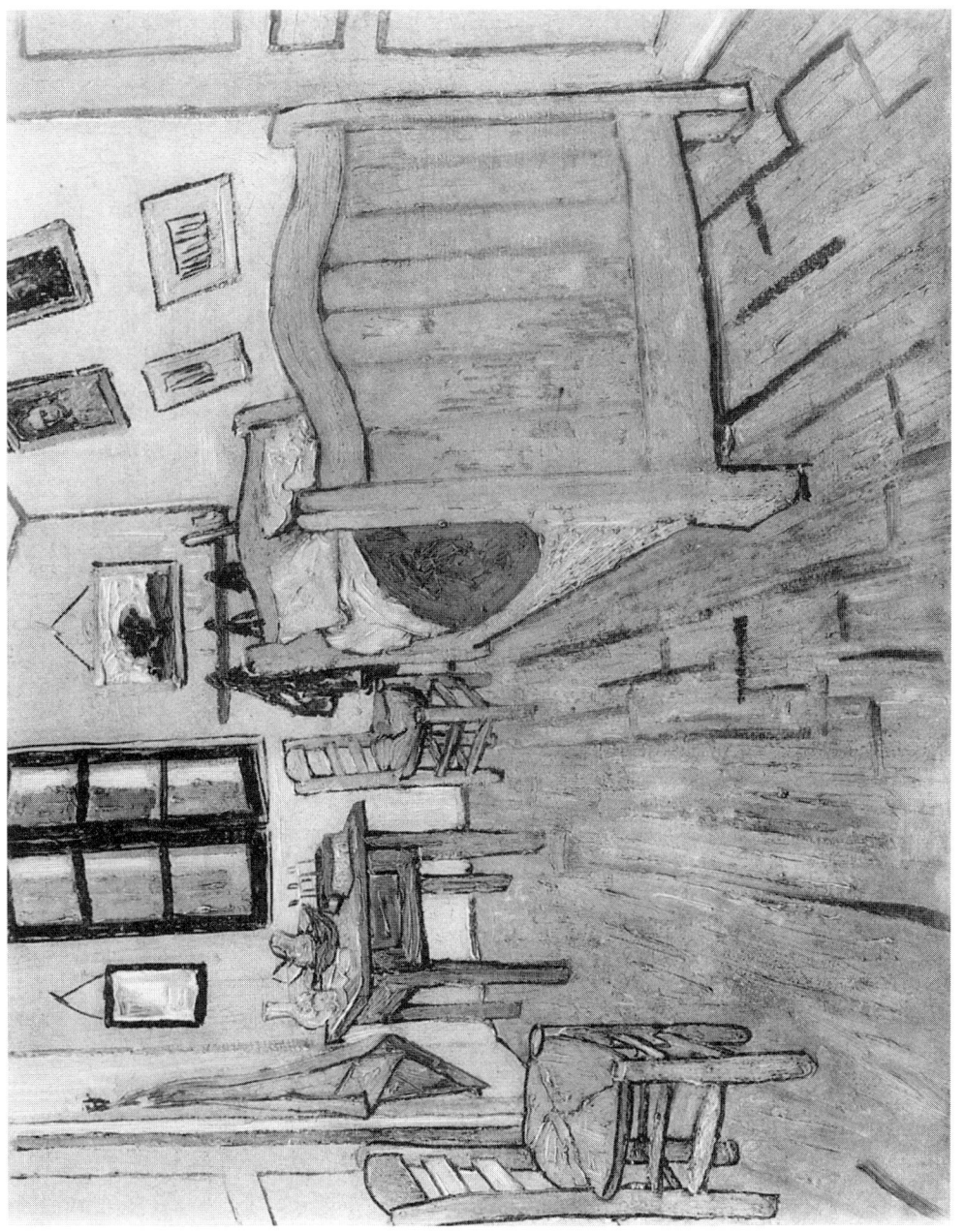

VAN GOGH'S BEDROOM AT ARLES

I have had gas put into the studio so that we shall have a good light in winter.

Maybe you'll be disappointed with Arles if you come while the *mistral* is on: but wait . . . It's only in the long run that one succumbs to the charm of the place.

You won't find the house as comfortable yet as we will gradually try and make it. There are so many expenses! And it can't all be done at one go. Still I believe that once here you will be seized, like me, with a passionate desire to paint the autumnal effects, in the intervals between the *mistral,* and that you will understand why I insisted on your coming here, at least while we have such lovely weather.

Till we meet then,

Yours,

Vincent.

---

[1] *Vide Letters to Theo* No. 555 (headed "October"): "Gauguin writes that he has already sent off his trunk and promises to come about the 20th of this month, that is within a few days."

[2] Gauguin was still suffering from dysentery.

[3] *"sans emmerdement."*

[4] *i.e.,* in February 1888.

[5] Plates 29 and 30; de la Faille No. 484. *Letters to Theo* No. 554 (written in October 1888) also contains a drawing of this composition.
In the light of Letter 608 it is clear that it cannot be de la Faille No. 483, as this is a smaller version ("a reduction" to 10 or 12) and was done at St. Rémy; de la Faille No. 482 is closer to this in style than to 484, and as we know he repeated the picture twice while he was at St. Rémy this seems the correct dating.

XXIII

A Note from GAUGUIN *to* EMILE BERNARD, *written from Arles in November* 1888 *and here published for the first time.*[1]

Purple vines forming triangles against the upper part which is chrome yellow.[2] On the left a Breton woman of Le Pouldu[3] in black with grey apron. Two Breton women bending down in blue and light green dresses with black bodice : in the foreground pink soil and a poor woman with orange coloured hair, white blouse and skirt (*terre verte* with white added). All this done with bold outlines enclosing tones which are almost similar and laid on thickly with a knife on coarse sack-cloth.

*   *   *

It is a view of a vineyard which I have seen at Arles. I have put Breton women into it—*accuracy* doesn't matter. It's my best canvas this year and as soon as it is dry I will send it to Paris. I have also done one of a café which Vincent likes a lot and myself[4] less. Actually it's not my subject and the vulgar local colours don't suit me. I like it in the work of others but myself I am always afraid. It's a matter of education and one cannot start all over again.

At the back red wall paper and three prostitutes: one bristling with curl-papers, the second seen from behind wearing a green shawl. The third in a scarlet shawl: on the left a man asleep. A billiard table—in the foreground a rather carefully executed figure of an Arlésienne with a black shawl and a white tulle[5](?) front. Marble table. Across the picture runs a streak of *blue smoke* but the figure in the foreground is *much too* orthodox. But still!

PLATE 31

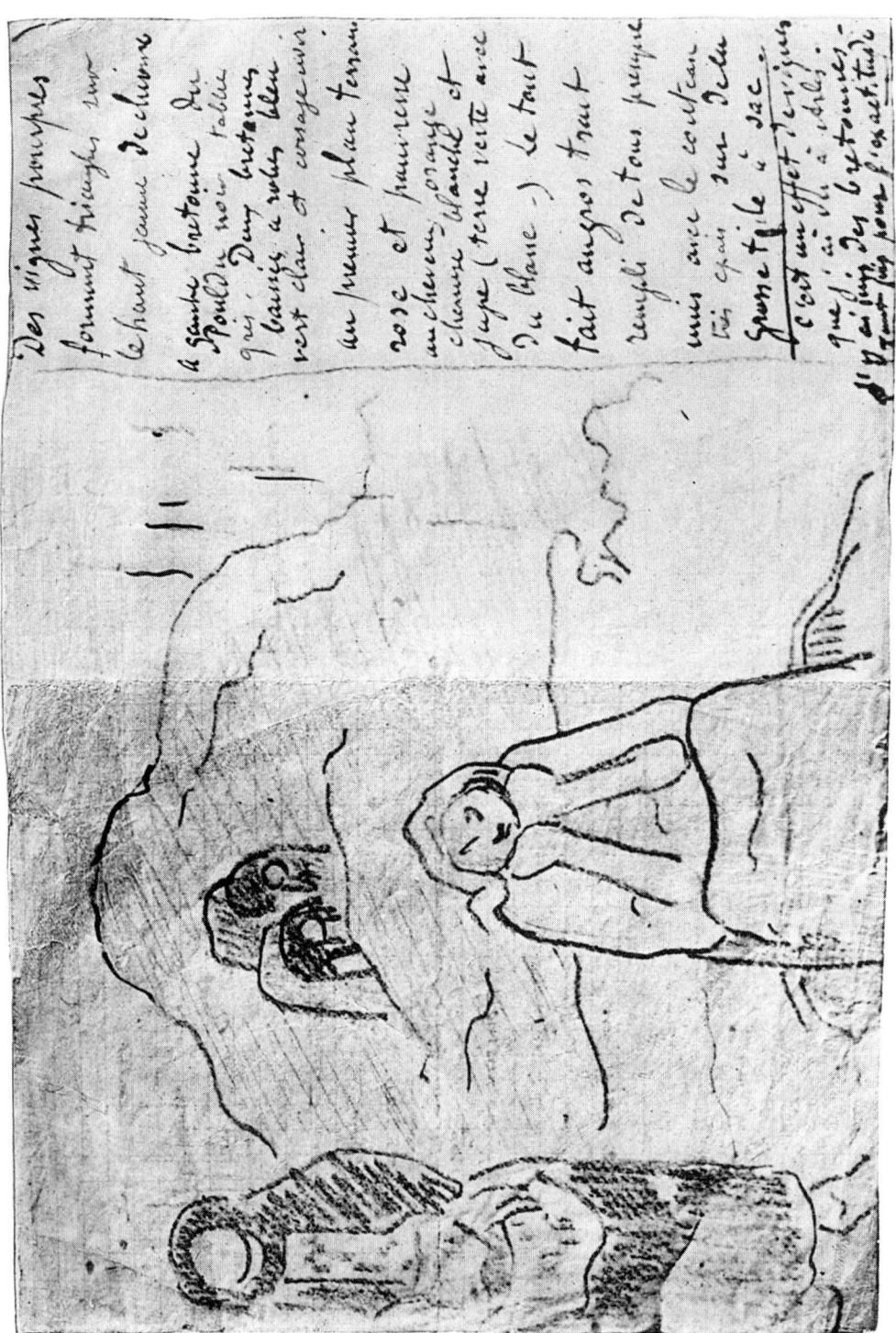

FACSIMILE FROM LETTER XXIII

PLATE 32

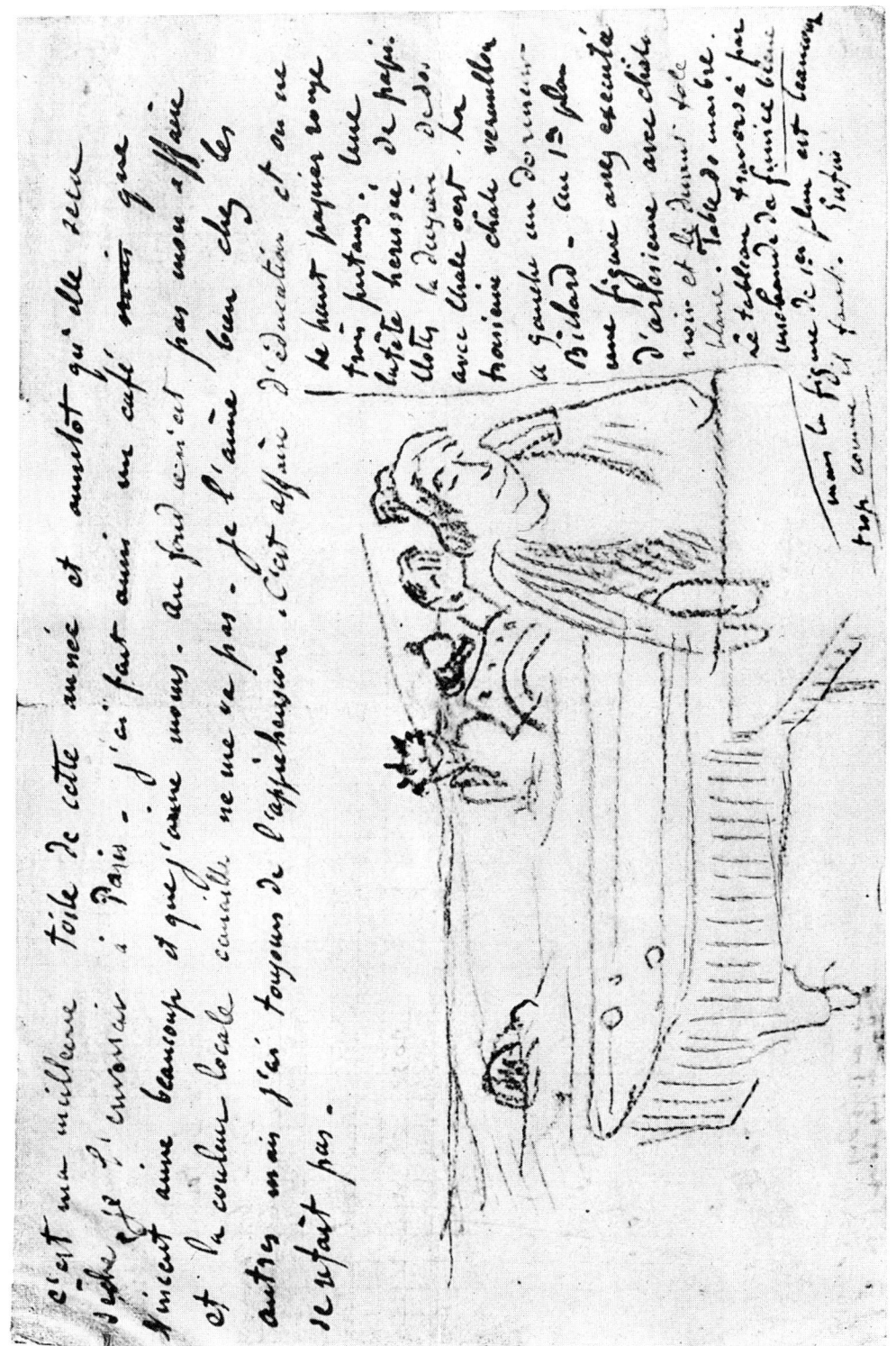

FACSIMILE FROM LETTER XXIII

¹ The two drawings, one on each side of the sheet, are obviously of paintings referred to in *Letters to Theo* No. 559 (headed "November") and which reads: "Just now he [Gauguin] has in hand some women in a vineyard, altogether from memory, but if he does not spoil it or leave it unfinished it will be very fine and very unusual. Also a picture of the same night café that I painted too."
This letter is written on a sheet of white paper measuring $4\frac{3}{4} \times 7\frac{1}{4}$ inches (12 × 18 cm.) ruled with a network of small squares.

² Plate 31.

³ A small fishing village in Brittany not far from Pont-Aven. The picture in question is one of the ones that precipitated the row between Gauguin and Bernard, for the composition is taken almost direct (though reversed) from a picture painted by Bernard in the early summer of 1888, which was subsequently given to Gauguin (after it had brought about a scene in the Pension Gloanec) and taken by him to Arles.

⁴ Plate 32. Gauguin, with his usual inaccuracy, gives a false idea of the *Café de Nuit*: cf. LETTERS XVI, XVIII and XIX. The figure in the foreground is one of the series of drawings of Arlésiennes by Gauguin which inspired Vincent to produce the pictures catalogued by de la Faille Nos. 540–543.

⁵ This word is illegible.

CHRONOLOGY

1853 *March 30th*: Vincent Willem van Gogh born at the parsonage of Groot-Zundert in Brabant

1857 *May 1st*: Theodorus van Gogh, his brother, born

1868 *April 28th*: Emile Bernard born at Lille

1869 *July*: Vincent van Gogh enters the firm of Goupil, art-dealers in The Hague

1873 *January*: Theo sent to Brussels to learn to become an art-dealer

May: Vincent transferred to London

1874 *October*: Vincent transferred to Paris

1875 *January*: Vincent returns to London

May: Vincent returns to Paris

1876 *April*: Vincent dismissed from Goupil's

May: He becomes a teacher in a school at Ramsgate

1877 *January*: Back in Holland; employed in a bookshop in Dordrecht, subsequently begins studying for the Theological Seminary

1878 *November*: Volunteers for evangelical service in the Borinage

1880 *October*: In Brussels studying anatomy and perspective; the friendship with Rappard begins

1882 *January*: In The Hague; begins studying painting with Anton Mauve

1883 *December*: Returns to live with his family and continues painting

1885 *May*: *The Potato Eaters*

November: Moves to Antwerp

1886 *March*: Arrives in Paris and stays with Theo in the Rue Laval; joins the studio of Cormon

April: Emile Bernard sees him for the first time at Cormon's

June: Vincent and Theo move to a new apartment in the Rue Lepic

1887 *April*: Gauguin and Laval leave for Panama; Vincent meets Emile Bernard one day at Père Tanguy's, they exchange pictures and their friendship begins

June: The exhibition in the Café Tambourin; Vincent spends much time painting with Bernard at Asnières

1888 *January*: Gauguin and Laval return to Paris from Martinique

February: Gauguin goes to Pont-Aven; Vincent suddenly departs to Arles

February 20th: He takes a room over the Restaurant Carrel in Arles

March: LETTER II

April: Pictures of *Orchards in bloom*; LETTER III; Bernard sets out on his annual trip to Brittany; LETTER IV

May: Vincent rents 4 rooms in a house on the Place Lamartine, Arles; *View of Arles, Still Life with Coffee-Pot*; LETTER V

June: Spends a week at Saintes-Maries; *Boats on the Beach; Boats on the Sea; Houses at Saintes-Maries*; LETTER VI; *The Sower*; giving drawing lessons to Milliet; Gauguin is ill; LETTER VII; *Portraits of the Zouave*; LETTERS VIII & IX

July: Drawings of the view around Montmajour; LETTER X; LETTER XI; 9 sketches of Provence sent to Bernard as an exchange; *Portrait of Mousmé*; LETTERS XII & XIII

August: *Portraits of Roulin*, the postman; LETTER XIV; Bernard joins Gauguin at Pont-Aven; *Men unloading a sand-barge*; LETTER XV; Theo passes on a legacy from an uncle and Vincent at last has enough money to furnish and decorate his house; *The Sunflowers* begun

September: *The Night Café*; Vincent moves into the "Yellow House"; LETTERS XVI, XVII & XVIII; further exchanges with Bernard

October: Receives portraits from Bernard and Gauguin, also Bernard's *"At the Brothel!"*; *The Night Café* (small version) painted from memory for Bernard; LETTER XIX; *The Bedroom at Arles*; Theo sells two pictures for Gauguin and the latter decides to go and join Vincent in Arles; LETTER XXII (to Gauguin)

October 20th: Gauguin arrives; Portraits of *L'Arlésienne* begun

November: LETTER XXIII (from Gauguin to Bernard)

December: Growing tension between Vincent and Gauguin

December 24th: Vincent in a fit cuts off an ear; he is put in hospital

1889 *January 7th*: Vincent leaves hospital; the *Berceuses, Portrait of Dr Rey*

February: After another attack Vincent returns to hospital for a few days

April: Theo gets married

May 8th: Vincent enters St. Rémy asylum; he works in the garden

June: He is allowed to work outside the walls; *Cypresses; Wheatfields*

July: A visit to Arles

July 7th or 8th: Seized with a fit while outdoors painting the *Entrance to a Quarry*

August: He begins to work again, but only indoors

September: "Working without a break" in his room; copies after Millet, Daumier and Delacroix; repetitions of the *Bedroom at Arles; Wheatfield with reaper*

October: Starts working again outside; LETTER XX; *The Ravine; Olive Trees*

November: *The Asylum Garden;* LETTER XXI

1890 *January*: Theo's son born

January 29th: A visit to Arles is followed by another fit

February 24th: Seized with a fit while staying for two days at Arles; taken back to St. Rémy

March: One of his pictures sold for 400 francs at the Vingtistes Exhibition in Brussels

May: Sufficiently recovered to resume work; *Irises; Roses; Self-Portraits*

May 17th: Leaves St. Rémy; spends a day or two with Theo in Paris

May 21st: Goes to Auvers to Dr. Gachet; *Portraits of Dr. Gachet and his daughter; Landscapes at Auvers*

June: A visit from Theo; spends a few days with Theo in Paris

July 27th: He shoots himself

July 29th: He dies

1891 *January 25th*: Theo dies

1892 An Exhibition organised by Bernard at the gallery of M. Lebarc de Boutteville in Paris

SELECT BIBLIOGRAPHY

LETTRES DE VINCENT VAN GOGH À EMILE BERNARD, ed. Ambroise Vollard, Paris 1911. This volume contains five prefaces by Emile Bernard:
1 specially written for the volume.
2 reprint of an article from the *Mercure de France* April 1893.
3 reprint of a preface to a collection of the *Letters from Vincent to Theo*: first published in the *Mercure de France* August 1893.
4 a preface written in 1895 to the first projected (though never published) edition of the *Correspondence of Vincent van Gogh* (ed. *Mercure de France*).
5 reprint of a biographical notice from a volume in the series *Hommes d'aujourd'hui* (ed. Vanier), written in 1891.

À EMILE BERNARD: LETTRES DE VAN GOGH, GAUGUIN, ETC., Vol. I; Editions de la Rénovation Esthétique, Tonnerre 1926; limited to 500 copies. This contains a selection of the letters in the present volume, and another biographical preface by Emile Bernard.

THE LETTERS OF VINCENT VAN GOGH TO HIS BROTHER 1872–1886, with a memoir by his sister-in-law, J. van Gogh-Bonger. 2 vols. London, Constable & Co. 1927; New York and Boston, Houghton Mifflin Co. 1927.

FURTHER LETTERS OF VINCENT VAN GOGH TO HIS BROTHER 1886–1889. 1 vol. London, Constable & Co. 1929; New York and Boston, Houghton Mifflin Co. 1929.

THÉO VAN GOGH: LETTRES À SON FRÈRE VINCENT: with a note on Mme. J. van Gogh-Bonger, by V. W. van Gogh; ed. Maatschappij Tot Verspreiding Van Goede En Goedkoope Lectuur, Amsterdam 1932. This volume contains 41 letters from Theo and his wife Jo to Vincent, covering the period from October 19th 1888, until July 14th 1890.

LETTERS TO AN ARTIST: from Vincent van Gogh to Anton Ridder van Rappard, 1881–85; translated by Rela van Messel; Constable & Co., London, 1936; Viking Press, New York 1936.

L'OEUVRE DE VINCENT VAN GOGH: CATALOGUE RAISONNÉ, by J. B. de la Faille; 4 vols.; van Oest, Paris and Brussels 1928.

111

DE HOLLANDSCHE PERIODE IN HET WERK VAN VINCENT VAN GOGH, by Dr. Walter Vanbeselaere; ed. Wereldbibliothek, Amsterdam 1938.

L'EPOQUE FRANÇAISE DE VINCENT VAN GOGH, by J. B. de la Faille; ed. Bernheim-Jeune, Paris 1927, on the occasion of a retrospective van Gogh exhibition.

VAN GOGH'S GREAT PERIOD: ARLES, ST. RÉMY, AUVERS, by Doctors Scherjon and Gruyter; a catalogue, ed. "De Spieghel" Ltd., Amsterdam 1937.

PERSÖNLICHE ERINNERUNGEN AN VAN GOGH, by E. H. Du Quesne-van Gogh; ed. R. Piper & Co, Munich 1911.

VAN GOGH (Great Lives, No. 29), by Peter Burra; Duckworth, London 1934.

VAN GOGH, by Michel Florisoone; Libraire Plon, Paris 1937.

VINCENT VAN GOGH, by Walter Pach; Artbook Museum, New York 1936.

VINCENT VAN GOGH, with an introductory note by Wilhelm Uhde; Phaidon Press, Vienna: George Allen and Unwin, London 1936: Oxford University Press, New York 1936.

VAN GOGH, by Charles Terrasse; Libraire Floury, Paris 1935.

VAN GOGH, by Théodore Duret; Bernheim-Jeune, Paris 1910, 1919, 1924.

LA VIE TRAGIQUE DE VINCENT VAN GOGH, by Louis Piérard; Crès, Paris 1924.

VINCENT VAN GOGH: A BIOGRAPHICAL STUDY, by Julius Meier-Graefe; translated by John Holroyd Reece. 2 vols.; Medici Society, London and Boston 1922 and 1926: Payson & Clarke, New York 1928: Harcourt Brace, New York 1933: Michael Joseph, London 1936. The original German text was published by the Piper Verlag, Munich in 1912 and 1922.

VINCENT VAN GOGH, by Paul Colin; Medici Society, London 1922: Dodd Mead & Co., New York 1926.

VINCENT VAN GOGH, by Anthony Bertram; "The Studio," London (World's Masters series) 1929 and 1934.

VAN GOGH, by T. W. Earp; Nelson, London 1934.

STRINDBERG UND VAN GOGH, by Karl Jaspers; ed. Ernst Bircher, Leipzig 1922.

VINCENT VAN GOGH IN DER KRANKHEIT, by Walter Riese; ed. J. F. Bergmann, Munich 1926.

VINCENT VAN GOGH: catalogue of an exhibition, with an introduction and notes by Alfred H. Barr, Jr.; Museum of Modern Art, New York 1935.

CATALOGUS VINCENT VAN GOGH, with foreword and notes by W. Steenhoff; Stedelijk Museum, Amsterdam, no date. A list of works in the collection of V. W. van Gogh and now *in bruikleen* to the Gemeente of Amsterdam.

VINCENT VAN GOGH: a catalogue of paintings in the Kröller-Müller Stichting, The Hague, no date.

VAN GOGH: SA VIE ET SON OEUVRE: catalogue of an exhibition at the Paris Exposition 1937; composed by MM. Florisoone and Rewald; ed. *L'Amour de L'Art*.

COMPARATIVE TABLE OF LETTER NUMBERS

Present Edition	Vollard Edition
I	I
II	II
III	III
IV	IV
V	V
VI	VI
VII	VII
VIII	XI
IX	XII
X	XVIII
XI	XIII
XII	X
XIII	VIII
XIV	IX
XV	XIX
XVI	XVI
XVII	XIV
XVIII	XV
XIX	XVII
XX	XX
XXI	XXI
XXII	XXII
XXIII	Not included

EMENDATIONS TO THE PUBLISHED TEXT

For various reasons, it was considered impossible in 1911, to publish the text of van Gogh's letters *in toto*: this, therefore, is the first edition (even though in translation) of the complete text. So I take this opportunity of listing the emendations and additions which should be made to the version published by M. Vollard in 1911. I have here preserved the order of the letters as they were published in that volume: the corresponding number in the present edition can be found by reference to the Table of Comparison.

LETTER I

p 73, l 3, Légendes Russes *written without capital letters, therefore, should not be printed in italics.*

p 73, l 4, *read* Eug., *not* Eugène Delacroix.

p 74, l 9, Car il est . . . *should begin a new paragraph.*

p 75, l 17, égoïste *should read* égoïsme; *omit the colon.*
The letter is simply signed Vincent.

LETTER II

p 76, l 15, *for* cinq, *read* 5.

p 76, l 16, *for* quatre, *read* 4.

LETTER III

p 78, l 8, *for* fait, *read* fasse.

l 15, *for* blancs, jaunes, *read* blancs-jaunes; *omit* Je.

l 17, *No paragraph.*

p 79, l 1, *in* caractéristiques *Vincent has omitted the second* c.

l 2, *for* oignons verts, *read* oignons, ail.

l 10, *for* et, *read* ou.

l 23, *add* Te souhaite bon voyage—poignée de main en pensée, Ton ami, Vincent.

LETTER IV

p 80, l 12, *for* six, *read* 6.

l 24, *for* Rend, *read* rend.

p 81, l 14, *for* et des couleurs, *read* et couleurs.

l 15, *for* n'y restera, *read* y restera.

l 19, *should read* Ai 9 vergers . . .

p 82, l 16, *add* Je dois justement lui écrire.

l 20, midi, *written with capital* M.

The letter ends, t.à.t. Vincent.

LETTER V

p 83, l 6, *for* tout une tribu indigène, *read* tout une tribu d'indigènes.

l 7, *read as follows* disons une fois par mois on mangeait un individu—qu'est-ce que ca fait! !

l 12, *from* pour se . . . *to end of paragraph written in brackets.*

l 13, Une femme *should not be in italics, only the word* sublime *is underlined.*

l 15, *omit the word* et.

l 18, Quelque *written without capital letter.*

l 20, *for* t . . ., *read* tirent; *for* c . . ., *read* coups.

l 22, *for* m . . ., *read* maquereau.

p 85, l 1, *for* trois, *read* 3.

p 86, l 2, *add* Puis deux études de bords de routes—après—faites en plein mistral.

l 3, *omit* un.

Letter signed simply Vincent.

LETTER VI

p 88, l 9, *after* simple cobalt, *a full stop. Then with a new paragraph* Alors pourquoi . . .

l 11, *omit question mark.*

p 89, l 7, *for* quatre, *read* 4.

l 10, *after* Saintes-Maries *a comma, then continue,* et pour y arriver ai traversé en diligence la Camargue avec des vignes, des landes, des terrains plats comme la Hollande. Là, à Saintes-Maries il y avait . . .

Bottom line: for tout à toi, *read* t.à.t. Vincent.

LETTER VII

p 90, l 15, *for* vingt cinq, *read* 25.

l 16, *for* trente cinq, *read* 35.

l 20, *omit the word* un.

p 91, *bottom line: for* trente, *read* 30.

p 92, l 24, *read* C'est pourtant vrai une raison de ne pas travailler . . .: *no paragraph.*

p 93, l 1, *for* ce pays, *read* ce pays-ci: *omit the word* c'est.

l 23 *should read* Faire de la peinture et baiser beaucoup n'est pas compatible, le cerveau s'en affaiblit. Voilà qui est bien emmerdant.

p 94, l 26 *should read* . . . m'arrive ici d'avoir en demandant à la poste même en cas de doute été trompé en affranchissant.

Bottom line: for tout à toi, *read* t.à.t. Vincent.

p 95, l 2, *for* je n'en doute, *read* j'en doute.

    l 20, *for* vingt, *read* 20.

p 97, l 30, *for* p . . ., *read* putain.

p 98, l 20, *for* fort simple, *read* fort fort simple.

    l 25, *for* Rembrandt van Ryn, *read* Rembrandt Harmensz van Ryn: *for* et large autant que Hals, *read* et sain autant que Hals.

p 99, *bottom line*: *for* tout à toi, *read* t.à.t. Vincent.

LETTER IX

p 100, l 17, *for* trois, *read* 3; *for* quatre, *read* 4.

p 101, l 8, *for* une sorte d'oeuf, *read* une forme d'oeuf.

p 102, l 19, *should read* Pourquoi dis-tu que Degas bande mal? Degas vit . . .

    l 21, *for* b . . ., *read* baisait.

    l 23, *for* X . . ., *read* Degas.

    l 26, *for* b . . . et b . . ., *read* bander et baiser.

    l 28, *for* b . . ., *read* bander.

    l 29, *for* b . . ., *read* baiseur.

    l 30, *for* b . . ., *read* baiser.

p 103, l 1, *for* b . . ., *read* baise; *for* en ne b . . ., *read* en ne baisant.

    l 16, *for* b . . ., *read* bander.

    l 17, *for* b . . ., *read* baiser.

    l 25, *for* b . . ., *read* baisait.

p 104, l 9, *for* m . . ., *read* maquereau.

    l 10 *should read* . . . à la satisfaction des organes génitaux de la putain . . .

    l 12, *for* p . . ., *read* putain.

p 105, l 2, *for* Tout à toi, *read* t.à.t. Vincent.

LETTER X

p 106, l 16 *should read* . . . as-tu jamais bien regardé le "Boeuf" ou "l'intérieur d'un boucher" au Louvre?

p 107, l 9, *before* jaune citron, *insert* bleu.

    l 24 *should read* (. . . sujets bibliques) voilà le seul qui, par exception aie fait . . .

p 108, l 22, *for* douze, *read* 12.

Bottom line: *for* Tout à toi, *read* t.à.t. Vincent.

LETTER XI

p 109, l 5, *for* Saint Luc, *read* Saint Luc etc.

p 111, l 23 *should read* . . . Conditions supérieures et changées d'existence, existence changée par . . .

p 112, l 17, *for* Eugène, *read* Eug.

p 113, l 18, *for* dix, *read* 10.

p 114, l 2 *should read* Vas-tu en Afrique ou pas? Est-ce que les années comptent double dans ton cas en Afrique ou non? Surtout cherche . . .

l 14, *for* quatre, *read* 4; *for* six, *read* 6.

l 20, *add* t.à.t. Vincent.

LETTER XII

p 115, l 2, *for* ton sonnet, *read* ton dernier sonnet.

l 14, *for* Crau (Camargue), *read* Crau et Camargue.

p 116, *after* l 13 *add two new paragraphs*: Si tu voulais je destinerais à un échange avec toi la tête du Zouave que j'ai peinte.

Seulement je n'en parlerai qu'en cas que je puisse en même temps te faire vendre quelquechose.

l 31 *should read* . . . que des paysages. Des paysages . . .

p 117, l 12, *add* t.à.t. Vincent.

LETTER XIII

p 119, l 2, *for* neuf, *read* 9.

after l 22 *add a new paragraph*: Involontairement les oeuvres forment "groupe" "série".

p 120, *bottom line*: *add* t.à.t. Vincent.

LETTER XIV

p 121, l 8 *should read* . . . en plus enfin ce qu'il y aurait en plus!

l 10 *should read* . . . soit juste. Mais moi je te vois . . .

p 122, l 23, *for* où bon te semble, *read* au bordel.

p 123, *bottom line*: *add* t.à.t. Vincent.

LETTER XV

p 126, l 24, *van Gogh uses the non-existent word* invraisemblabilités *which has been corrected to* invraisemblances.

p 126, l 31, *for* deux, *read* 2.

p 127, l 2, *The whole passage from* dans les croquis . . . *to* . . . chez mon frere! *should be enclosed in brackets.*

p 127, l 5, *for* fort curieux, *read* fort fort curieux.

l 18, *for* collection Bing, *read* publication Bing.

l 20, *add* t.à.t. Vincent.

LETTER XVI

p 128, l 5, *for* ainsi, *read* aussi.

p 129, l 5, *for* deux francs cinquante, *read* 2.50 frs.

l 7, *for* tente *read* tenterait.

l 9 *should read* pas ici se faire . . .

p 130, *bottom line*: *add* t.à.t. Vincent.

118

LETTER XVII

p 131, l 12, *for* Au B . . ., *read* Au Bordel.

l 14, *for* t . . ., *read* travailler.

l 18, *for* b . . ., *read* bordel.

p 132, l 1, *for* b . . ., *read* bordel.

l 4, *for* p . . ., *read* putain.

l 6, *for* m . . . *read* maquereau; *for* p . . ., *read* putain.

p 133, l 33 *should read* Peutêtre ici aussi, je n'en . . .

p 134, *bottom line, for* Tout à toi, *read* t.à.t. Vincent.

LETTER XVIII

p 135, l 7, *read*

"Des tapis velus
De fleurs et de verdures tissus".

de Crevelli ou Virelli peu importe.

p 137, l 2, *should read* . . . part et d'autre. Et . . .

Bottom line: *for* Tout à toi, *read* t.à.t. Vincent.

LETTER XIX

I have not been able to examine.

LETTER XX

p 141, l 29, *should read* . . . pourriez-vous, qui l'aurez vue . . .

p 142, *bottom line*: *for* Tout à toi, *read* t.à.t. Vincent.

LETTER XXI

p 143, l 18 *should read* . . . les gens l'ont senti. Après cela viendrez-vous nous renouveler les tapisseries moyen-age?

p 144, l 15, *for* il faut te le dire, *read* faut-il dire le mot.

l 16, *Vincent here wrote by mistake the word* affection *not* affectation.

p 145, l 19, *for* mêlée, *read* mâle.

l 25 *should read* . . . à saisir des étoiles trop grandes et nouvel échec, et j'en ai assez.

p 149, l 13 *should read* . . . sites ici. Viens de faire 5 toiles de 30 . . .

l 21 *should read* . . . qui est empâtée et faite sur place et non de répétition à hâchures où l'effet est plus faible. Je voulais faire cela en plein soufre.

l 27, *for* tout à toi, *read* t.à.t. Vincent.

There is very little punctuation throughout: I have therefore not noted the liberties that have been taken in this direction.

LETTER XXIII (*in the present volume only*).

Des vignes pourpres formant triangles sur le haut jaune de chrôme. A gauche bretonne du Pouldu noir tablier gris. Deux bretonnes baissées à robes bleu vert clair et corsage noir: au premier plan terrain rose et pauvresse aux cheveux orange, chemise blanche et jupe (terre verte avec du blanc). Le tout fait au gros trait rempli de tons presque unis avec le couteau très épais sur de la grosse toile à sac.

*   *   *

C'est un effet de vignes que j'ai vu à Arles. J'y ai mis des bretonnes—tant pis pour *l'exactitude*.

C'est ma meilleure toile de cette année et aussitôt qu'elle sera sèche je l'enverrai à Paris. J'ai fait aussi un café que Vincent aime beaucoup et que j'aime moins. Au fond ce n'est pas mon affaire et la couleur locale canaille ne me va pas. Je l'aime bien chez les autres mais j'ai toujours de l'appréhension. C'est affaire d'éducation et on ne se refait pas.

Le haut papier rouge trois putains: une la tête hérissée de papillotes la deuxième de dos avec châle vert. La troisième châle vermillon: à gauche un dormeur. Billard— au 1er plan une figure assez exécutée d'arlésienne avec châle noir et le devant tulle (?) blanc. Table de marbre. Le tableau traversé par une bande de *fumée bleue* mais la figure de 1er plan est beaucoup *trop comme* il faut. Enfin!

INDEX

Africa, 36, 39, 40, 41, 48, 77, 78, 80, 81
Aix en Provence, 14, 24, 57
Algeria, 27, 28, 37
Anquetin, Louis, 12, 13, 21, 90, 101
    paintings: *Harvest*, 38
        The Peasant, 55
Antibes, 47
Arles, 8, 9, 22, 28, 31, 32, 35, 53, 58, 73, 76,
        80, 83, 104, 105, 106
    letters from: 22–91, 104–107
Asnières, 46, 49, 82
Balzac, Honoré de, 64, 70
Baudelaire, Charles, 10, 41, 59, 63, 66, 67, 96
Bernard, Emile, a note on, 12–15
    and Cézanne, 5, 14–15
    at Asnières, 49
    at Pont-Aven, 23, 74, 76, 82
    correspondence with Gauguin, 13
    exhibition at the Café Tambourin, 21
    health of, 20, 21, 28, 40, 41, 48, 70, 80–81,
        101
    his father, 81, 82, 83
    his ideas stolen by Gauguin, 13
    "Jean d'Orsal", 15
    Lautrec's portrait of, 12
    "Ludovic Nemo", 13
    military service, 20, 21, 27, 39–40, 47, 70,
        77, 80–81, 83, 93, 101
    on original publication of letters from van
        Gogh, 6–8
    paintings: *A Brothel*, 50, 51, 53
        Adoration of the Magi, 96
        Annunciation, 96
        At the Brothel (sketches), 88, 91
        Breton Studies, 55
        Breton Women, 70, 83, 96, 102
        Christ carrying the Cross, 97
        Decoration of a Chapel at Tantah, 14
        Early work, 12
        Frescoes at Samos, 14
        Lechery, 66
        "peintures pétroles", 13
        Portrait of a Woman, 32, 33
        Portrait of Gauguin, 88

Prostitutes, 80
Self-Portrait, 19
Sketch of a Brothel, 39
Sketches sent to van Gogh (1888), 59
*Still lifes and Portrait of the artist's
    grandmother*, 68–9, 70
Studies of Pont-Aven, 85
The Artist's Sister, 97, 102
The Tree, 66
Three Trees, 97
poetry, 15, 26–7, 31, 33, 41, 48, 50, 52, 54, 88
quarrel with Gauguin, 107
the Rénovation Esthétique, 15
value of his opinion on van Gogh, 1, 15
views on Louis XIV, 47, 49
Blanc, Charles, 60, 62
Blanc, Louis, 62
Bol, Ferdinand, 66
Botticelli, Sandro, 44
Boulevard Montmartre, 41, 43
Boussod and Valadon, 43
Brittany, 12, 25, 73, 93
Bürger, W. = Thoré, E. J. T., *q.v.*
Burnett, Robert, 13
Café Tambourin, 20, 21
Café Volpini, 13
Camargue, The, 35, 50, 53, 57
Canvas, sizes of, 38, 39, 43, 48, 83, 88, 92,
    100, 104
Carcassonne, 95
Carrel, Restaurant, 28
Cézanne, Paul, 3–4, 5, 14, 50, 57, 72, 73,
    103
Cimabue, 35, 69
Collège Ste. Barbe, Paris, 12
Concarneau, 12
Constant, Benjamin, 47, 49
Cormon, Fernand, 12
Corot, Jean Baptiste Camille, 93
    Mount of Olives, 100
Courbet, Gustave, 59, 67, 69, 70, 73
Cranach, Lucas, 26, 44, 47
Crape-prints, Japanese, 22, 23
Crau, The, 50, 53, 54, 57, 58

Crivelli, Carlo, 54, 56
Dante, 65
Daudet, Alphonse, 29, 34, 41
Daumier, Honoré, 64, 69, 71, 72, 96
da Vinci, Leonardo, 67
de Chamaillard, 84, 86, 89
de Chavannes, Pierre Puvis, 49, 69, 73
    St. John Baptist, 47
Degas, Hilaire-Germain-Edgar, 7, 59, 69–70,
    73
de Haan, 9
de Hooch, Pieter, 66
Delacroix, Eugène, 3, 4, 19, 44, 47, 60–61,
    64, 67, 70–71, 78, 100
    *Christ in the Boat on the Sea of
      Gennesaret*, 46
de Maupassant, Guy, 41, 43
de Monfried, Daniel, 13
de Musset, Alfred, 66
de Rotonchamps, 23
d'Orleans, Charles, 56
d'Orsal, Jean=Bernard, Emile, *q.v.*
Dürer, Albert, 26, 47
Escalier, Patience, 76
Expressionism, 4
Fantin-Latour, Henri-Jean-Ignace-Théodore,
    20, 21
Fabritius, Carel, 66
Fort, Paul, 6
Fromentin, Eugène, 36, 37, 60, 78
Garnier, Charles, 93
Gauguin, Paul, 38, 83, 90, 92, 96, 97, 100, 101
  a note to Bernard, 106
  and Cézanne, 5
  at Arles, 94, 97
  at Pont-Aven, 23, 40, 68
  debt to the South, 78, 79
  first meeting with Bernard, 12–13
  illness, 35, 55, 105
  inaccuracy of, 8
  ingratitude to van Gogh, 8–10
  on Bernard's portrait of his sister, 97, 102
  paintings: *A Night Café*, 106, 107
    Caricature of Vincent van Gogh, 85, 86
    Christ in the Garden of Olives, 102
    Negresses (Martinique), 30, 33
    Portrait of Bernard, 88
    Women in a Vineyard, 106, 107
  portrait of, suggested by van Gogh, 77, 79
  proposed visit to Arles, 80
  quarrel with Bernard, 107

  source of his ideas, 13
  sunflowers, use of in painting, 76
  Synthetism, 13
  with Bernard, 74, 76
  with van Gogh at Montpellier, 98
Gérôme, Jean Léon, 36, 37, 78
Giotto, 35, 68–9, 75, 98
Giotto, school of, *Death and Assumption of the
    Virgin*, 103
Gloanec, Madame, 23
Goncourt, Edmond and Jules, 69, 73
Goupil's, 9, 43
Goya, 63, 67
Gruyter, Dr., 25, 86, 87
Guilds of St. Luke, 58
Guillaumin, Armand, 19
Hague, The, 42
Hals, Frans, 64–5
Holbein, Hans, 47, 69
Holland, 12, 35, 38
Huysmans, Joris Karl, 39, 43
Ile St. Louis, 15
Impressionism, 3, 10, 21, 56, 57, 73, 97
Ingres, Jean Auguste Dominique, 3
Isaacson, 95
Israels, Josef, 38, 42
Italy, 14
Japan, 22–3, 41, 104
  art of, 54, 59
  exchange of pictures by artists in, 85
  styles in painting, 34, 35
Jaspers, Dr., 11
Lautrec, *see* Toulouse-Lautrec
Laval, Charles, 13, 23, 84, 86, 89
Le Pouldu, 106, 107
Lille, 12, 14
Loti, Pierre, 41, 43
Louis XIV (Le Roi-Soleil), 8, 47, 49
Louvre, The, 48, 63–4
Luther, Martin, 47
Maes, Nicholas, 66
Marquesas Islands, 30
Marseilles, 14, 24, 27, 28, 55
Martinique, 13, 56, 79
Maus, Octave, 103
Mauve, Anton, 38, 42
Michelangelo, 15, 65, 67
Millet, Jean François, 38, 42, 44, 59, 64, 93,
    96, 100
Milliet, a Zouave officer, 39, 48, 49,
    77

Monet, Claude, 41, 42, 47, 73, 103
Monticelli, 57, 78
Montmajour, 56
Montpellier, 98, 103
Moret, 84, 86, 89
Naples, 14
Nemo, Ludovic=Emile Bernard, *q.v.*
Normandy, 12
North Sea, 28
Nuenen, Brabant, 76
Ostade, Adrian van, 63, 66, 67
      The Painter's Family, 63, 67
Panama, 56
Paris, 12, 40, 46, 55, 88, 90, 104
  Exposition of, (1889), 13, 93
  Opera House, 95
Pension Gloanec, Pont-Aven, 13, 23, 107
Picasso, 11
Pierrefonds, Chateau of, 95
Pissarro, Camille, 21
Pointillism, 19, 21
Pont-Aven, 13, 22, 23, 40, 68, 72, 75, 76, 77,
      85, 89, 92
Potter, Paulus, 48, 49, 57–8, 66
Poussin, 4
Puget, 67
Puvis, *see* de Chavannes
Raphael Santi, 65
Read, Herbert, 5
Rembrandt Harmensz van Ryn, 11, 44, 48,
      57–8, 59–61, 63–66, 67, 68
    paintings: *Self-Portrait*, 60, 62, 75
          The Slaughtered Ox, 59, 61
Renoir, 3, 73, 103
Rénovation Esthétique, founded by Bernard, 15
Richepin, Jean, 48
Roulin, postman of Arles, 71, 73
  his wife, 102
Rousseau, Théodore, 42
Rubens, Peter Paul, 67, 70
Russell, John, 29, 37, 42
Ruysdael, Jakob, 58, 66
St. Rémy, 92, 95, 96, 98, 105
  letters from, 92–103
Saintes-Maries de la Mer, 35, 37, 42, 53
Sargent, John Singer, 103
Scherjon, Dr., 25, 86, 87
Schuffenecker, Emile, 13, 23
Segatori, Agostina, 21
Sérusier, 23
Seurat, 4, 21, 104

Sickert, W. R., 103
Signac, Paul, 19, 21
Silvestre, Théophile, 64, 67
Spain, 14
Synthetism, 13, 23
Tangier, 24
Tanguy, Julien ("Père Tanguy"), 12, 14, 71, 73
Tantah, 14
Tarascon, 57
Teersteeg, 9
Terborch, 66
      Peace of Münster, 63
Thannhauser, Henry, 29, 37, 42
Thomas, Parisian art-dealer, 55, 56
Thoré, Etienne Joseph Théophile, 60, 62
Tolstoy, Count, 19
Tonkin, 39
Toulouse-Lautrec, 12, 21, 103
Vallette, Alfred, 6
van Delft, Vermeer, 66, 68
      Lady reading a letter, 59, 62
Van Dyck, Sir Anthony, 69
van Eyck, Hubert and Jan, 26, 44
van Gogh, Theo, 1–2, 7, 8, 9, 13, 41, 43, 47,
      50, 53, 55, 85, 90, 92, 96
van Gogh, Vincent,
  at St. Rémy, 92, 95
  attachment to Gauguin, 8–9
  exhibition at the Café Tambourin, 21
  first meeting with Bernard, 12
  health, 27, 28, 30, 95, 98, 100
  importance of his correspondence, 2–3
  letter to Gauguin, 104–5
  Letters to Theo, 1 *et seq.*
  mental condition of, 10–11
  on abstraction in art, 97, 103
  on Bernard's and Gauguin's studies of
      Christ, 97, 102
  on collaboration in art, 57
  on cost of living at Arles, 77, 80, 82, 83–4
  on cost of painting, 40
  on exchange of pictures among artists, 84–5
  on freemasonry among painters, 84
  on olive trees, 93, 97–8
  on painting from models, 89–90
  on painting in a wind, 39
  on patience, 41
  on "present day painting", 34
  on Provence, 92–3
  on reading the Bible, 44 *et seq.*, 51, 99, 100
  on use of black and white, 34, 35, 39

on the teaching of Christ, 44–5, 51
paintings: *A field of young wheat*, 99
    A ravine, 94
    A reaper in a wheatfield at St. Rémy,
       100–101, 103
    A small garden with flowers, 84
    Bedroom at Arles, 2, 104
    Blossoming fruit trees, 24, 25
    Boats on the beach at Saintes-Maries, 35
    Bull-fights, 25
    Christ with the Angel in Gethsemane, 89
    decorations for the Café Tambourin, 21
    Entrance to a quarry, 92, 94
    Green meadow with dandelions, 24, 25
    Houses at Saintes-Maries, 36, 37
    Landscape: "A stretch of country", 84
    Landscape: "In Mistral", 84
    Man and Woman in the Night Café,
       88–9
    Men unloading a Sand Barge, 74, 76,
       84, 89
    Mousmé, 61, 62, 74, 76
    Olive groves, 100
    *Ploughed fields with background of
       mountains*, 92, 94
    Poet against a starry sky, 89, 91
    Portrait of Père Tanguy, 73
    Portrait of Patience Escalier, 74, 76
    Provençal orchards, 24, 25, 27, 29
    Red Sunset, 90,
    Roulin, his wife and children, 74, 76
    Self-portrait, 84
    sketches in letters, 22, 35, 36, 37, 39
    sketches of Provence, 57
    Star-spangled sky, 24, 25
    Starry Night, 85
    Still life of peasant shoes, 84
    Still life with Coffee Pot, 31, 37
    Still life with Lemons in a Basket, 31

    Sunflowers, 75, 76, 85, 86
    The Drawbridge at Arles, 22
    The Furrows, 85
    The garden of the asylum at St. Rémy,
       10, 98, 99, 102
    Milliet, 77
    The Night Café, 78, 84, 88, 91
    The Old Mill, 89
    The Poet's Garden, 85, 87
    The Postman Roulin, 71, 73
    The Potato Eaters, 9, 74, 76
    The Sower, 38, 39, 42
    The Street, 85
    The Summer Evening, 50, 53
    The Vineyard, 85
    The Zouave, 46, 47, 49, 51
    Thistles with Butterflies, 84
    van Gogh's House at Arles, 85
    View of Arles, 31–2
    View of Arles at Sunset, 39, 43
    Wheatfield with Labourer and Train,
       54
    Wheatfields, 51
    Woman reading a Novel, 97
    Woman rocking a Cradle, 97
  personality of, 1
  perspective frame, 39, 43
van Gogh-Bonger, Madame, 2
van Rappard, 9
Velazquez, Diego Rodriguez de Silva y, 44,
    60, 63, 64
Venice, 14, 15
Vingtistes, The, 103
Viollet-le-Duc, Eugène-Emmanuel, 93
Vollard, Ambroise, 7
Watteau, Antoine, 4, 67
Whistler, James Abbot M'Neill, 103
Yellow House, Place Lamartine, Arles, 30, 32
Zola, Emile, 4, 64, 65

DOVER BOOKS ON ART, ART HISTORY

THE ART OF BOTANICAL ILLUSTRATION: AN ILLUSTRATED HISTORY, Wilfrid Blunt. (Available in U.S. only.) (27265-6)

CHRISTIAN AND ORIENTAL PHILOSOPHY OF ART, Ananda K. Coomaraswamy. (20378-6)

AMERICA'S OLD MASTERS, James T. Flexner. (27957-X)

HISTORY OF AMERICAN PAINTING, VOL. 2: THE LIGHT OF DISTANT SKIES (1760–1835), James T. Flexner. (25708-8)

VISION AND DESIGN, Roger Fry. (40087-5)

FORM, FUNCTION & DESIGN, Paul Jacques Grillo. (20182-1)

MODERN MEXICAN PAINTERS, MacKinley Helm. (26028-3)

MODERN ARTISTS ON ART, SECOND ENLARGED EDITION, Robert L. Herbert (ed.). (41191-5)

A HISTORY OF ENGRAVING AND ETCHING, Arthur M. Hind. (20954-7)

ART AND GEOMETRY, William M. Ivins. (20941-5)

CONCERNING THE SPIRITUAL IN ART, Wassily Kandinsky. (23411-8)

POINT AND LINE TO PLANE, Wassily Kandinsky. (23808-3)

LANGUAGE OF VISION, Gyorgy Kepes. (28650-9)

THE ART-MAKERS, Russell Lynes. (24239-0)

THE LIFE OF WILLIAM MORRIS, J. W. Mackail. (28793-9)

VINCENT VAN GOGH: A BIOGRAPHY, Julius Meier-Graefe. (25253-1)

PAINTERS OF THE ASHCAN SCHOOL, Bennard B. Perlman. (25747-9)

PERSPECTIVE IN ARCHITECTURE AND PAINTING: AN UNABRIDGED REPRINT OF THE ENGLISH-AND-LATIN EDITION OF THE 1693 "PERSPECTIVA PICTORUM ET ARCHITECTORUM," Andrea Pozzo. (25855-6)

PAINTERS ON PAINTING, Eric Protter. (29941-4)

THE ILLUSTRATOR AND THE BOOK IN ENGLAND FROM 1790 TO 1914, Gordon N. Ray. (26955-8)

RODIN ON ART AND ARTISTS, Auguste Rodin. (24487-3)

THE SEARCH FOR FORM IN ART AND ARCHITECTURE, Eliel Saarinen. (24907-7)

THE SENSE OF BEAUTY, George Santayana. (20238-0)

PICASSO, Gertrude Stein. (24715-5)

THE GENTLE ART OF MAKING ENEMIES, James A. McN. Whistler. (21875-9)

PRINCIPLES OF ART HISTORY, Heinrich Wölfflin. (20276-3)

DOVER BOOKS ON FINE ART

FRENCH SATIRICAL DRAWINGS FROM "L'ASSIETTE AU BEURRE," Stanley Appelbaum (ed.). (23583-1)

BEARDSLEY'S LE MORTE DARTHUR: SELECTED ILLUSTRATIONS, Aubrey Beardsley. (41795-6)

THE RAPE OF THE LOCK, Aubrey Beardsley and Alexander Pope. (21963-1)

BLAKE'S "AMERICA: A PROPHECY" AND "EUROPE: A PROPHECY" FACSIMILE REPRODUCTIONS OF TWO ILLUMINATED BOOKS, WITH 35 PLATES IN FULL COLOR, William Blake. (24548-9)

SONGS OF INNOCENCE, William Blake. (22764-2)

THE ART OF BOTANICAL ILLUSTRATION, Wilfrid Blunt. (Available in U.S. only.) (27265-6)

GRAPHIC WORLDS OF PETER BRUEGEL THE ELDER, Peter Bruegel. (21132-0)

SELECTED FABLES OF JEAN DE LA FONTAINE, illustrated by Alexander Calder. (21878-3)

A CÉZANNE SKETCHBOOK: FIGURES, PORTRAITS, LANDSCAPES AND STILL LIFES, Paul Cézanne. (24790-2)

THE POSTERS OF JULES CHÉRET: 46 FULL-COLOR PLATES AND AN ILLUSTRATED CATALOG RAISONNÉ. SECOND, REVISED AND ENLARGED EDITION, Jules Chéret and Lucy Broido. (26966-3)

REGINALD MARSH'S NEW YORK/PAINTINGS, DRAWINGS, PRINTS AND PHOTOGRAPHS, Marilyn Cohen. (24594-2)

ILLUSTRATIONS AND ORNAMENTATION FROM THE FAERIE QUEENE, Walter Crane. (40274-6)

CONTEMPORARY POLISH POSTERS IN FULL COLOR, Joseph Czestochowski (ed.). (23780-X)

THE NOTEBOOKS OF LEONARDO DA VINCI. (Available in U.S. only.) (22572-0, 22573-9) 2-vol. set

DALÍ ON MODERN ART, Salvador Dalí. (29220-7)

THE DORÉ ILLUSTRATIONS FOR DANTE'S DIVINE COMEDY, Gustave Doré. (23231-X)

DORÉ'S ILLUSTRATIONS FOR ARIOSTO'S "ORLANDO FURIOSO," Gustave Doré. (23973-X)

DORÉ'S ILLUSTRATIONS FOR "IDYLLS OF THE KING," Gustave Doré. (28465-4)

LONDON: A PILGRIMAGE, Gustave Doré and Blanchard Jerrold. (22306-X)

THE COMPLETE ENGRAVINGS, ETCHINGS AND DRYPOINTS OF ALBRECHT DÜRER, Albrecht Dürer. (22851-7)

THE ILLUMINATED BLAKE, David V. Erdman. (27234-6)

ERTÉ'S FASHION DESIGNS, Erté. (24203-X)

ERTÉ GRAPHICS, Erté. (23580-7)

NEW ERTÉ GRAPHICS IN FULL COLOR, Erté. (24645-0)

AMERICAN CIRCUS POSTERS IN FULL COLOR, Charles Philip Fox. (23693-5)

NOA NOA: THE TAHITIAN JOURNAL, Paul Gauguin. (24859-3)

THE GIBSON GIRL AND HER AMERICA, Charles Dana Gibson. (21986-0)

THE LIFE OF WILLIAM BLAKE, Alexander Gilchrist. (40005-0)

THE DISASTERS OF WAR, Francisco Goya. (21872-4)

ECCE HOMO, George Grosz. (23410-X)

MODERN MEXICAN PAINTERS, MacKinley Helm. (26028-3)

ENGRAVINGS BY HOGARTH, William Hogarth. (22479-1)

THE DANCE OF DEATH, Hans Holbein the Younger. (22804-5)

100 GREAT ANTIQUE AUTOMOBILES IN FULL-COLOR PRINTS, Clarence P. Hornung. (26841-1)

WILL BRADLEY: HIS GRAPHIC ART, Clarence P. Hornung (ed.). (20701-3)

THE GRAMMAR OF ORNAMENT, Owen Jones. (25463-1)

100 DRAWINGS, Gustav Klimt. (22446-5)

PRINTS AND DRAWINGS OF KÄTHE KOLLWITZ, Käthe Kollwitz. (22177-6)

THE ART NOUVEAU STYLE: A COMPREHENSIVE GUIDE WITH 264 ILLUSTRATIONS, Stephan Tschudi Madsen. (41794-8)

DRAWINGS: THEMES AND VARIATIONS, Henri Matisse. (Available in U.S. only.) (28520-0)

DEGAS, Julius Meier-Graefe. (25702-9)

MEDIEVAL AND RENAISSANCE TREATISES ON THE ARTS OF PAINTING, Mary P. Merrifield. (40440-4)

GREAT BALLET PRINTS OF THE ROMANTIC ERA, Parmenia Migel. (24050-9)

ORNAMENTATION AND ILLUSTRATIONS FROM THE KELMSCOTT CHAUCER, William Morris. (22970-X)

MUCHA'S FIGURES DÉCORATIVES, Alphonse Mucha. (24234-X)

THOMAS NAST'S CHRISTMAS DRAWINGS, Thomas Nast. (23660-9)

PENNELL'S NEW YORK ETCHINGS: 90 PRINTS, Joseph Pennell. (23913-6)

ROBERT HENRI: HIS LIFE AND ART, Bennard Perlman. (26722-9)

PAINTERS OF THE ASHCAN SCHOOL: THE IMMORTAL EIGHT, Bennard B. Perlman. (25747-9)

THE PRISONS, Giovanni Battista Piranesi. (21540-7)

THE COMPLETE ETCHINGS OF REMBRANDT, REPRODUCED IN ORIGINAL SIZE, Rembrandt van Rijn. (28181-7)

FREDERIC REMINGTON: 173 DRAWINGS AND ILLUSTRATIONS, Frederic Remington. (20714-5)

GREAT LITHOGRAPHS BY TOULOUSE-LAUTREC, Henri de Toulouse-Lautrec. (24359-1)

RENOIR: AN INTIMATE RECORD, Ambroise Vollard. (26488-2)

THE DOVER ART LIBRARY